URBAN MONK

EXPLORING KARMA, CONSCIOUSNESS, AND THE DIVINE

Urban Monk – Exploring Karma, Consciousness, and the Divine

Copyright © 2013 Pankaj Srivastava (Gadadhara Pandit Dasa)

Printed in the United States of America

Book cover design by Olia Saunders
(portfolio.oliasaunders.com)

Editing by Chelsea Pula

First Edition: July 2013

ISBN 13: 978-0615844237

This book is dedicated to my parents, who exemplify loyalty, dedication, and sacrifice.

Many planks and sticks, unable to stay together, are carried away by the force of a river's waves. Similarly, although we are intimately related with friends and family members, we are unable to stay together because of our varied past deeds and the waves of time.

- Srimad Bhagavatam 10.5.25

CONTENTS

PREFACE

In 2008, while walking in a park in Paramus, New Jersey, a friend of mine suggested that I write a book because I could offer some unique wisdom to those seeking spiritual guidance. In the moment, it sounded appealing, but having never written anything other than school papers, I had no interest in writing a book. I didn't write for leisure and never even kept up with a diary or journal.

Nevertheless, there was something that appealed to me in the idea. Since a lot of what I do is talk to people and listen to the challenges in their lives, I thought it only appropriate that I take time to acknowledge and meditate on my own challenges. If I wrote everything down, I could take time and reflect on the journey that had brought me to this stage in my life. I never knew how to answer when people asked me, "Why did you become a monk?" How could I summarize 27 years of life experiences in a short conversation? Writing it out might sort out my thoughts and allow me to share them with others. So, I gave it a shot. I sat down and started writing, but after a few pages I lost interest and gave up the project.

In early 2011, after having been a monk for almost 12 years, something changed. This time when I set out to write, the words flowed through me easily. Looking through the results—this book— I realize that my life hasn't always been smooth or simple. I've lived in many different cities and several countries. My finances have not always been stable. I faced a large crisis in my early 20s that left me feeling disconnected from the people around me. As I took inventory of my life experiences, I tried to understand how all of what happened has affected me, positively and negatively, and made me the person I am today.

As a monk, I've taught in universities, in yoga studios, and in people's homes about the importance of taking our spiritual lives seriously. The spiritual philosophy of the *Bhagavad Gita* and the practice of meditation have given meaning and focus to my life. If my journey can inspire others to take up spiritual life, then it would be worth it to share my personal story.

INTRODUCTION

It's 5:00 a.m. in New York's Lower East Side and the alarm on my iPhone goes off. I have two choices: turn off the alarm and go back to sleep, or wake up and get ready for the morning services. Most of the time, I choose the latter. For 12 years, I slept on a two-inch thick and two-foot wide sleeping mat, but have recently upgraded to an actual bed with a mattress. I unzip myself out of my sleeping bag, offer prayers to our previous teachers, stuff my sleeping bag into its stuff-sack, and roll out of bed, hoping none of the other monks have beaten me to the bathroom. After brushing my teeth, responding to the call of nature, showering, applying the sacred markings that represent the footprint of God on my forehead, arms, and torso, putting on my saffron colored robes, and slipping on my crocs, I walk down the stairs to the temple on the third floor.

When most people envision a monastery, they picture an East Asian structure with sloping rooftops and serene, high-peaked mountains in the background. It's probably surrounded by lush greenery where monks are peacefully sitting in a lotus posture meditating and praying. Our monastery is a six-story brownstone on the same block as several nightclubs and bars, a tattoo shop, a funeral home, and a drag queen cabaret. Down on the corner of First Avenue and Second Street sits the laundromat where monks and hundreds of Lower East Side residents do their laundry. Beyond that lies the F train subway station on First and Houston. You'll get funny looks if you try to pronounce Houston like the Texan city because New Yorkers call it Howston. There's hardly a time of the day when people, bikes, cars, taxis, buses, trucks, and ambulances, aren't zooming by in a mad rush. On the Avenue, I quite often hear people yelling and screaming at each other in a drunken stupor as the bars are closing and evacuating their guests. Often times one can hear beer bottles smashing against the street and see red and blue lights flashing as the police appear on the scene to break up a brawl. This is where I chose to practice a monastic life. It's obvious to me that here is where spirituality is needed the most.

Upon entering the temple room, my nose is filled with the smell of freshly burning incense. The temple walls are covered with large, colorful paintings of scenes of the holy village of Vrindavana and its residents, the incarnation Chaitanya, and prominent teachers from our tradition. At the front of the temple, towards the Avenue, there's a hand-carved wooden altar that is about six feet wide and whose tip touches the ceiling. The room is equipped with ceiling fans and is lit with recessed lighting. I offer my respects to the other monks and building residents who have decided to attend the morning ceremony by bowing down and touching my forehead to the hardwood floor. I then put my hands into my saffron-colored, stitched-cloth bag, reach for my sacred beads, and softly begin to chant and meditate on the names of God.

After the morning ceremony comes to a close around 9:00 a.m., I eagerly make my way down to the first floor for breakfast. The menu varies from American – oatmeal, pancakes, muffins, and smoothie – to a more traditional Indian lineup – *poha* (spiced flat rice), *upma* (cream of wheat with mixed vegetable), or a *sabji* (spiced vegetables), and sometimes, an Indo-American combination with a side of fruits.

After breakfast, I go to my room, flip open my Macbook, check my email and log onto Facebook. I then begin to plan my day and rest of the week by looking at my calendar and to-do list. The day's activities can include cooking classes and meditation sessions, or lectures at Columbia, New York University, local high schools, yoga studios, or a friend's home. Some evenings and afternoons are spent meeting with working professionals from my spiritual community; others are spent with students, staff, or faculty from local universities. The meetings can be very unpredictable.

In my early days of monastic life, when people asked to meet with me I automatically assumed they wanted to talk only about their spiritual lives. I thought they would strictly ask me questions about the teachings of Hinduism and how they can be exercised. Over time, I've found that most people want to discuss issues from their personal lives and hope to find a spiritual perspective on their dilemma and suffering. These days when I receive a meeting request, I know to mentally prepare for just about anything. Before the session, I meditate and pray that I can have the sensitivity to understand the individual's plight and inspire them with the right words. I've learned to ask people to give me an idea of what they want to discuss so I can be mentally prepared to discuss delicate topics.

Early on in my monastic life, around 2002, a young working professional of the Hindu faith reached out to me. He wanted me to organize and host a memorial ceremony at the temple for a friend who had recently passed away. It would be my first time organizing and hosting something like this. I asked him to bring a picture of his friend so we could place it near the altar. When I asked how his friend died, he said "suicide." She was in her late 20s, had a successful career and had a lot of friends. No one saw it coming. One morning she got ready to go to work, but never made it out the door. She hung herself from the ceiling fan. I wasn't sure if I was ready to deal with the heaviness of the situation. I prayed that I would be able to say the right words to comfort him and all of the friends he had invited. I looked to the *Bhagavad Gita* to guide me in my speech.

The gathering was primarily for the friends who knew her from the New York City area. Her family lived in a different part of the country and couldn't come to the ceremony. About thirty-five friends of all different ethnicities and faiths attended. After everyone sat down, I spoke from chapter two of the *Bhagavad Gita*, which describes the eternal nature of the self. I explained that although it would be difficult and painful for us to no longer be in the physical presence of the individual, we could take solace in understanding that the soul is eternal and indestructible—that it can't be burned by fire, withered by wind, or moistened by water. I explained that it's never too late for each of us to offer prayers for the deceased because only the physical body has ceased to exist, not the actual person.

I also suggested that amidst our busy schedules and personal ambitions, we find time to check in on each other's lives. Everyone faces challenges in their lives, and we want to connect with them before they reach a breaking point. Sometimes, a simple phone call can prevent a disaster. Everyone seemed to appreciate the messages and the ceremony. Afterward, the young man thanked me for the talk.

Interactions and situations with students weren't any less intense. After attending one of my meditation sessions, a graduate student of psychology requested to meet. We met on campus and she hesitatingly said, "I'm not sure how much I should say to you." I simply told her to speak as much as she felt comfortable speaking. She explained that she was trying to keep her head above water between a rigorous academic schedule and a job; that she was in the middle of going through a nasty divorce and that her soon-to-be ex-husband was dragging her through the mud. He was trying to prevent her from getting custody of their child. When she had initially asked to talk to me, she had a pleasant smile and demeanor, but in the middle of her story, she broke down in tears. I had assumed she had more questions about the meditation techniques I had taught. I would have never guessed that it would be such a heavy discussion. I spent most of the time just listening to her since I knew that that was all I could really to do help. It's hard not to feel a bit helpless in these situations. I encouraged her to stay strong and recommended a daily meditation practice as a way to keep the mind clear of negative thoughts. The meditation would also give strength to balance her work, school, and personal life. I also suggested she maintain whatever other spiritual practices she performs so that her soul could continue to experience nourishment through this turbulent time.

Not all interactions were or are so intense and grave. One student from New York University emailed me asking if we could meet. Since it was early in the fall and the weather was warm, we decided to meet in Washington Square Park. He told me he was thinking of going into the field of medicine. However, he was very uncomfortable with the animal experimentation that he was going to have to do and was considering changing majors. He was of the Hindu faith and wanted to know what Hinduism said about experimenting on animals. I told him that ultimately this was a decision that he would have to make in consultation with his academic advisors and family members. Since he wanted to specifically know the Hindu perspective, I told him that Hinduism states that we shouldn't harm any living creature unless it poses a threat to us because all creatures have the right to live out their lives like humans do. He said he felt the same and would consider more deeply which steps he should take next.

In addition to guiding people on a one-on-one basis, one of my big challenges as a monk living in an urban environment is to make spirituality not only relevant, but also accessible and entertaining. I decided that using Hollywood movies would be a powerful medium to introduce spiritual truths to a culture of people that constantly need sensory stimulation. My eyes were opened to the spiritual wisdom that was woven into the dialogue of the popular 1999 sci-fi movie *The Matrix*. Like Arjuna in the *Bhagavad Gita*, Neo seeks answers about his duty and his life. Both heroes know that a reality exists beyond their sensory experience, and both journey forward with a determination to distinguish reality from illusion. In time, I found more movies that explored the same tenets of ancient wisdom I wanted to teach, like *Inception, Contact, and A Beautiful Mind*. Each movie communicated certain themes that can be found within the spiritual texts of India. Many of these themes and concepts are from a very different paradigm and not easy to communicate. However, using familiar and popular movies, not only served as a wonderful tool, but also made the experience entertaining for the audience and for myself.

CHAPTER ONE

FILLING THE VOID IN THE HEART

Visiting India in 1987 was quite a culture shock. My family had left India in 1980 and hadn't been back since. We lived in Kanpur until I was five and spent another two years in Delhi. I was seven when we departed, and in the seven years that had passed I had grown from a small child into a young teenager while India faded further and further into my memory. Even though I could remember the poverty and filth, experiencing the sights, sounds, and smells again was overwhelming. Despite this, turning back was out of the question; our relatives were eager to see us, and my parents had never been away from their home for this long. I remember arriving at the Kanpur train station and being greeted by my family and childhood friends. They were so excited to see us coming from America, but I couldn't share their excitement. I felt so different from all of my cousins and former friends.

As my aunts, uncles, grandparents, and other family members, some of whom I remembered and some of whom I didn't, cheerfully greeted us, I tried my best to reciprocate. My parents had taught me from a young age that it was customary to touch the feet of any relative who was older than me. So, right at the train station, a whole foot touching extravaganza took place.

Other cultural differences were harder to adapt to. I remember that when my best childhood friend came to visit me, he put his arm around my shoulders and grabbed onto my hand and didn't let go. In India, this is a gesture of affection, but as an American I still felt uncomfortable being so close and holding hands with a friend. For him, however, it was the most natural way to express his affection towards an old friend.

Although most of my family could understand English they were too uncomfortable or shy to speak it. I felt the same way about Hindi; I could get by, but I was unable to express myself thoroughly. Growing up in Los Angeles wasn't very conducive to maintaining my native language. I think we were the only Indian family in all of Glendale, our hometown. As the days went by, I noticed that my cousins smiled every time I spoke Hindi. I eventually asked them out of curiosity why they were smiling and they told me I had an accent. I was shocked. I'd been speaking Hindi all my life. How in the world could I have an accent? After that incident I felt even more self-conscious, but I had to accept the fact that I did speak with an accent.

The whole two weeks I was in Kanpur, my family was always around us, taking care of us, feeding us, taking us for walks, and just trying their very best to make us all feel comfortable. I wasn't accustomed to getting this kind of attention and love. I remember it being a pretty festive visit. Relatives who I didn't know were coming and everyone who visited us brought some sweets or something to eat. My relatives cooked most of the meals personally, but on occasion we would order food from local restaurants. My parents had warned me to be moderate in my eating, but I think I had forgotten the advice. I was eating all the food my relatives brought. I was getting the royal treatment and a ton of attention. I loved it. I ate desserts made of milk, sweets soaked in sugar syrup, locally made ice creams, and of course lassis, sweet and creamy yogurt drinks. I dove into vegetable preparations made with deep fried panir (homemade cheese). My vegetarian relatives tolerated it while I scarfed down the tandoori chicken and kebabs. It was all so delicious!

It took about three days for my body to react to my gluttony and then I had to pay the price. My digestion decided that it could no longer deal with all the grease, spices, and sugar I had consumed and started the process of elimination. For the next three days, my stomach churned as I ran in and out of the bathroom flushing everything out. Many Indian toilets are inserted into the ground, which made the whole experience even more challenging because I wasn't used to squatting down. With my body completely drained, I either lied in bed fairly lifeless or hovered over the toilet. I had never gotten sick like this in my life, and I was learning the lesson of a lifetime. I have made about a dozen trips to India since this first trip in 1987, and I haven't yet been able to get through a single trip without at least some diarrhea, a cold, or a fever. Each trip gets easier than the one before. All that's required is a little restraint.

Our last day in India was very memorable. The taxi was waiting outside my grandfather's home. After a long session of goodbyes, we finally got into the car. As the taxi drove away, my mom cried harder than I'd ever seen her cry. I looked through the back window at my many family members and saw them crying. Seeing them, something came over me as well, and I began to cry like I never had before. I'd never felt such a rush of emotions overtake me.

We had left India in 1980 for greater happiness, and had achieved the American dream; however, as we drove away I realized that we had left behind something so valuable, something that all living creatures are looking for, and something that could never be replaced by any amount of wealth. Materially, I had everything I could want, but there was a certain warmth and love that was lacking deep within my heart which was filled in the two short weeks that I spent in Kanpur.

CHAPTER TWO

LIVING IN La La LAND

Growing up in America was filled with challenges. Even though my parents had sent me to an English-speaking school in India, I couldn't converse in the language, and as a result had trouble making friends. As an only child, I didn't have anyone who I could express my confusion and difficulties to and often felt lonely. Before settling into Glendale, California, where I would spend the next 11 years, we moved almost six times within four years. Every time I developed friendships, I had to leave them behind.

The *Bhagavad Gita* tells us that the material world is a temporary place in which nothing is permanent and that all we possess will eventually be taken away from us—every relationship, every possession, even our very bodies. Therefore, we shouldn't become overly attached to anything; otherwise, that very attachment will lead to pain and suffering.

Of course, the *Gita* isn't promoting indifference. We need to care for people in our lives and reciprocate with the love they have offered us and do everything we can to offer our service to those in need.

This is a concept that would make sense to me many years later when I started to explore my own faith in a serious way. At ten years old, it was just confusing. For the first five years of my life, I had lived in Kanpur, India. Then we moved to Delhi and lived there for two years, changing apartments twice, and then to America. After moving around, I lived in Glendale from age 10 until 21. There wasn't a specific place I could really call "home" and although I didn't realize it at the time, I was feeling disconnected.

My mom's side of the family practices strict vegetarianism. This meant that no meat, including fish and eggs, had ever entered her home. It was unthinkable. Things changed once we got to America. Since my dad was a world traveler, he had adapted to a meat-based diet. The day he introduced us to a non-vegetarian diet is etched into my head. We were sitting in a Wendy's and my father ordered a cheeseburger for me. I looked at it for a while before biting into it. Something about it didn't feel right, but I was only seven and too young to make any further calculations. After all, it was the American thing to do, and my parents wanted to fit in. Soon after that, meat, including beef, became a regular part of our diet. Busy at work, we had hardly any time for home cooked meals and ate out at a rotation of our favorite restaurants. There were no Indian restaurants in our area, but we loved American, Italian, Chinese, Mexican, and Middle Eastern cuisines. Other than breakfast, most of our lunches and dinners were non-vegetarian. A meal without meat almost didn't seem

. complete. Every time I visited India, I would try to convince my family and especially my cousins about the importance of eating meat. I'm glad they never took me seriously.

I don't know why my parents chose to live in Glendale. As far as I could tell, we were the only Indian family in a predominantly white city. It was about forty-five minutes from the nearest Indian town, Cerritos, and we would only go out there once every couple of months. In time, I grew distant from Indian and Hindu culture. I never really celebrated Holi, the festival of colors, or Diwali, the festival of lights, after coming to the States. As a child, I felt nostalgic for India at festival times.

I was the only "brown" kid in my elementary school. Once I heard a couple of girls call my skin dirty because of its brown complexion. Once, a kid in class drew a picture of an eight-armed goddess and claimed that it was my mother. It was hurtful and confusing, and I didn't know how to respond. It felt like everything about me was different. My nationality, skin color, and religion were different from those of other kids growing up in Glendale. Even the Indian food my mom packed wasn't the same as what everyone else was eating. I quickly switched to peanut butter and jelly or other types of sandwiches to try to fit in.

I hesitated to invite my friends over to my house because I was embarrassed about how "un-American" we were. My parents played Hindi songs and watched

Bollywood movies. More than that, our altar of worship had so many gods. Some had multiple hands and heads while others were half-human half-animal. I felt certain that I couldn't explain the foreign nature of the sights and sounds to my friends. I would become the laughing stock of the school if the word got out. I suppose the bi-cultural experience could have been a lot easier if we had lived in Cerritos with other Indians. For the most part, Indian culture was very foreign to the American public. Although I was happy about the awareness the 1982 movie "Gandhi" raised about India and its struggle for Independence, I wasn't thrilled when other kids referred to me as "hey Gandhi!" They obviously weren't attempting to glorify me. Once, as I was walking out of my fifth grade math class, a kid I didn't get along with called me Gandhi one too many times. I just wasn't able to tolerate it and right in class we got into a fight and somehow I ended up punching him in the face. Not very Gandhi-like of me! We both got sent to the principal's office. While we were sitting there waiting to talk to the principal, he turned to me and said "nice shot." However, things did get a lot easier as I transitioned into high school as there was greater ethnic diversity.

I think most Indian kids and perhaps other Asians who grew up in the 80s and 90s had a similar identity struggle. We all wanted to be American. We tried to dress like Americans, talk like Americans, listen to American music, and eat American food, but we still felt there was something different about us. By the time I was ten years old, I had already had a wide variety of life experiences that singled me out from my peers and distanced me from my home country. My identity splintered in two as I strove to be cool around my American friends and well-behaved for my parents.

There is a gap between Indians that immigrate to America and their American kids. For the most part, the parents were raised in a very conservative environment. They didn't stay out late, didn't date, and didn't rebel against their parents. Their marriages were often arranged by the time they reached their mid-twenties. After arriving into America, Indian parents expect their kids to abide by the same culture as the one they had grown up with in India. However, American culture is just the opposite of what they had experienced. When they try to enforce their Indian culture upon their children, there are clashes. It was very difficult for my parents to adjust to my staying out late at night with my friends. If it was up to them, they would want me home by 10:00 p.m., but on weekends, I wouldn't get home till 1:00 a.m. or later. My dad couldn't sleep until I was home and would stay awake worrying about me and waiting for me. I was fairly indifferent to their concerns.

The biggest complaint that the Hindu youth seems to have is that their parents just don't understand them. Once in a while I am invited to Hindu youth camps that take place during the summer seasons. The purpose behind these camps is to encourage the youth to remain Hindu. I usually give a few lectures about Hindu philosophy. The main concerns parents express is that they don't want their kids to become too American and lose their Hindu values. It's a valid concern, but completely unrealistic. It's practically impossible to live in a foreign culture and not be affected by it. Whenever parents express this to me, I always tell them that if they want their children to maintain Hindu values, then they have to set the proper example. From my observation, Indian parents who migrate to the U.S. have one goal in mind—financial stability. Therefore, the goal they have for their kids is education. Remaining Hindu is not their primary focus.

In India, other members of the family – aunts, uncles, and grandparents – all keep an eye on the children, but here in America, parents are busy working long hours and kids are busy studying or engaging in extracurricular activities with their friends. At least, that was the case with me. As Hilary Clinton once said, "it takes a village to raise a child." Well, in this case, the family left the village in India and came West. From what I understand, the parents' actual idea of being "Hindu" is that the kids should be obedient and live according to traditional Indian values. It doesn't really have anything to do with the spiritual philosophy and practices of the Hindu faith.

It was hard for me to understand at the time exactly how much my parents struggled to establish themselves in this country. During the first couple of years in America, while we were living in Culver City, which is a part of Los Angeles County, we hit a real low point financially, and my parents didn't even have enough money to buy milk for me. Since they were always busy working to try to put food on the table, I would go to school by myself and walk back home alone. There would be food waiting for me on the kitchen table, and I would heat it up and sit in front of the television and eat.

I watched so much TV that my parents actually threatened to remove it from the house. I must have been around ten years old, when one day, after coming home from school, I noticed the television was gone and I figured they actually followed through on their threat. When I called them at work and asked where the television was, they were confused. They said they didn't do anything with the television. I looked around and I noticed a few other things were also missing. We realized it was a burglary. Scared, I slowly walked through the rest of the house to see what else was missing. In retrospect, this was a really bad idea because the burglars could have still been in the house, but luckily they had already left. Almost everything we had of value—and it wasn't much—was stolen. My parents rushed home from work worried about my safety. Even though I had told them I was alright, they needed to see me with their own eyes to feel relief.

One of my dad's first business ventures, after coming to the United States, was an Indian furniture store in Los Angeles. It didn't last long and had to close down. That business swallowed up whatever little money my parents came to this country with. For the next couple of years, they would find and set up booths at different flea markets and swap meets. They would load up our '72 silver station wagon with all kinds of stuff— jewelry, clothing, and decorative items—from local wholesalers and sell them at different flea markets around the city. Eventually, they found out about the boardwalk on Venice Beach and rented a space there. They sold all kinds of gift and jewelry items; Indian brass figures and carvings, sunglasses, gold-plated jewelry, and even clothing.

Our booth was right across the basketball courts, where the movie *White Men Can't Jump* was filmed, and just a few steps away from Gold's Gym. I would go to the courts and shoot around with some black guys. They looked huge to me because I couldn't have been more than nine or ten years old, but they were really nice and welcomed me in. I would even call them uncle because in India, out of respect, you're supposed to refer to all adults as uncle or aunty. I spent my time playing basketball, swimming in the ocean, and riding my roller skates up and down the boardwalk. Venice beach turned out to be a very successful business venture for my parents. It did so well that my parents acquired a second booth a quarter-mile down.

It might have been these early years on the beach that developed my love for the ocean. That love only increased as I went beyond just body surfing the Southern California waves and started boogey boarding. Although later in high school my friends and I were never much for surfing, we took boogey boarding seriously. In summers, we'd sleep over one another's homes so we could wake up before the sunrise and get to the beach for the bigger morning waves. I even had a wetsuit so I could swim in the winter and fins to help me catch more waves.

During those years at Venice beach, I developed a good friendship with a kid named Kevin, who lived right on the beach. We would skate and ride our bikes together, but one day I went to his house and a stranger answered the door. When I asked if Kevin was home, the lady at the door told me they had moved. I was so saddened by this sudden news— Kevin's family didn't even tell me they were moving! As I walked back to my parents' booth, I tried to process that I would never see Kevin again.

My parents are incredibly resilient and determined people. Within five years of being in the country, they had established themselves comfortably. We purchased a small two-bedroom house in Glendale with a large front and backyard. My parents went from selling gift items at Venice Beach and other swap meet settings to running their own jewelry business from the garage of our Glendale house. By the time I was 12 we were pretty well off. It wasn't long before my father was traveling all over the country doing jewelry trade shows and amassing a large clientele for his business. He named his company after my birth name, Pankaj, and called it, "Pankaj International." In Sanskrit, Pankaj is another name for lotus flower.

We lived in that house for about five years when my dad, always the extravagant type, decided to construct his own home on the highest point of the Glendale hillside. The million-dollar house was so big that people thought it was an apartment building. It had six bedrooms, four and a half bathrooms, a massive living room and dining room, an outside Jacuzzi, and a 40-foot swimming pool with a small waterfall going down one side of the pool. Best of all, it had a beautiful view of all of Los Angeles county.

The house became a popular hangout spot for my parents' friends and for my friends. Since it was a bigger place, my parents could watch their Bollywood movies in their room. We had a separate room for the temple, and I had plenty of space for my friends to hang out without having the two cultures collide. During the summer time, my friends would come over to swim in our pool or just hang out and enjoy the view. At my parents' parties, they would listen to old and new Bollywood songs, but when my friends came over, we listened to hip-hop. My dad, a social drinker, had an eight-foot long bar where he showcased a large variety of alcoholic beverages with pride. He loved to play bartender and serve everyone drinks. I tried drinking a couple of times, but the taste never appealed to me. I also didn't have to worry about being pressured into it because most of my friends didn't drink.

I pretty much had everything I wanted. I had my own room overlooking all of Los Angeles with an attached bathroom. I had my own television, VCR, and stereo system, and on my sixteenth birthday I received a brand new car. Within a few years, we went from not having money for food to living the American dream.

I often wondered how it was that I landed in such a fortunate situation in life. After all, there were so many people living in poverty in India and in other parts of the world; how was it that my family was able to come to America and establish themselves? I did believe in the law of karma, but had little understanding of it. I always figured that I must have done something to deserve this, but I couldn't understand what.

High school, for me, was a sheltered experience. Being anxious of the drugs, smoking, and gang activity of my public middle school, I asked my parents to place me elsewhere. They put me in a small, Christian high school with a population of about 350 students. My graduating class of 1990 had a total of 80 students.

The kids there were nicer and I no longer felt stressed by bad influences.

In our free time, my friends and I loved to play sports, watch movies, and play video games. I loved playing tennis and volleyball, and I enjoyed watching football, but ever since Venice Beach my favorite sport had been basketball. I wasn't great at it, but I could hold my own on the court. I wasn't a great offensive player, but I excelled in the defensive position. Even though I wasn't that tall or wide—about 5' 8" and 145 pounds—I loved getting under the rim to get rebounds. I became a huge fan of the Los Angeles Lakers and tried to never miss a game. During the late 80s, the Lakers had the unstoppable big three: Magic Johnson, Kareem Abdul-Jabbar, and James Worthy. Watching them play was amazing. Magic was the tallest point guard the league had ever seen and could see over his defenders. Kareem had the unstoppable skyhook. I was devastated when I heard that Magic had contracted HIV and would no longer be playing. I moved into the monastery a couple of years after Kobe Bryant entered the NBA so I never had a chance to witness his rise to stardom. The Lakers were my favorite team, but I loved watching Michael Jordan play. He had a finesse that hadn't been seen before. His ability to hang in the air was a new phenomenon for the league. He dominated and owned the court like no one before.

I was introduced to tennis at an early age by one of my dad's friends. Tennis is more challenging mentally than basketball because there are no team members to bail one out in case one is having an off day. It is all up to the individual to lift oneself out of a slump and get his or her game back in gear. When I was 12 years old and living in Glendale, we had a park near our house with tennis courts where I would practice my serves in the mornings before school. I continued to play tennis on and off through high school and in my senior year won our high school tournament. Everyone was surprised because no one knew that I played.

The happy and carefree days of my life were about to come to a close and I was about to start the walk down the road of maturation. In 1992, my father's jewelry factory burnt down and he lost a tremendous amount of inventory. During this tragic event, one of his managers ran off with all of his business contacts and joined forces with a competitor, and as a result my dad lost most of his clients. Unable to pull things together, we eventually lost our house, cars, and practically all of the money we had saved. Hard times were on the horizon. Because things had come easy for me, I couldn't grasp the magnitude of what was happening. I had lived life in a bubble and hadn't personally experienced much hardship.

As our status dwindled, so did my sense of self. So much of my identity as a person was connected to the things we had accumulated and the status in society that we had developed. I wasn't the most motivated of individuals and never had much ambition to accomplish grand things in life. I had become dependent on the comforts my parents were providing and had expected that they would always be there. This sudden change created a lot of confusion in my life, about the present and future.

In 1993, it seemed as if there was nothing left for my father to pursue in Los Angeles and he was looking for an opportunity where he could once again make it big. In a desperate attempt to earn money, he decided to pursue an opportunity he had heard about from a friend, in the former Eastern block country of Bulgaria. Having just come out of communist rule, it was an open market and my dad wanted to capitalize on it. With so much uncertainty about my future, I lost all focus during my third year at Cal-State University of Los Angeles and decided to join my father in Bulgaria. I can still clearly remember standing in line to check out of school. It was a bit surreal. I knew this was going to be a major transition in my life, but I didn't have a clue what was in store.

I didn't tell my high school and college friends what I was going through and what I was about to do. I was embarrassed; I felt it was a failure on our part and it was hard to tell everyone that we had failed and were losing everything. As things tightened financially, I distanced myself from my friends because I no longer had money to go out to eat or watch movies. So, when we decided that we were going to leave the country, I packed whatever would fit in one suitcase and left California. Most of my friends had no clue what had happened. I told one friend that I was going abroad, but I only told him that it was to help my dad in his business. I didn't mention anything about the downturn our life had taken. For the most part, I had fallen off the face of the earth. I didn't want to be contacted, as I didn't really feel like explaining myself until we got back on our feet in some kind of "face-saving" way.

CHAPTER THREE

ENLIGHTENMENT IN BULGARIA

Within a couple weeks after leaving school, my mom and I flew to Bulgaria, leaving our home, cars, and other belongings at the mercy of the banks. As the flight was landing, I was taken aback at how depressing the city looked. All of the residential buildings looked identical and were approximately the same size and color.

My dad met us at the airport in Sofia and we drove about two hours to Plovdiv, where we arrived at our tiny, eight hundred square foot apartment. This was also quite a surprise, as the living room in our previous house in Glendale was bigger than this whole apartment. Everything here was technologically behind by about fifty years. I had to go to the post office to make an international call. Everything was incredibly difficult because of the language barrier, even purchasing groceries. Items had to be ordered from the person behind the counter, but they didn't speak English and the items were named differently from those in the English language. It was like I was starting all over again.

I had no clue how long I would be living in Eastern Europe, so I decided that I better start learning the language. Bulgarian was like nothing I had ever read, seen, or spoken before, but I had purchased a couple of English-to-Bulgarian books prior to coming to Bulgaria. Before I could learn any words, phrases, or sentences, I had to learn the characters of the alphabet, which resemble the characters in the Russian language. I don't think I've studied that hard for anything in my life. I guess sheer necessity allows one to accomplish things that would otherwise feel impossible. In a month, I was able to make purchases at the supermarket and after six months I was able to get around by taxi and have basic conversations with people.

I would sit on the balcony of our little apartment many times, staring out at the street and wondering where my life was going. At 21 years old, I'd dropped out of college, been thoroughly uprooted from my home, and moved to a new country. It was the second time in my life that I'd left my home behind and had to start fresh. Since I was older this time, the shift was drastic. I was in a very foreign country with a very different language and culture than what I was used to and I had absolutely no friends.

The country itself was in a state of despair having just come out of a communist regime. The people of Bulgaria were a little uncertain of where they stood, and they were quite suspicious of outsiders. There were hardly any foreigners in Bulgaria at the time, aside from some French-speaking African students. Being brown-skinned didn't help. I had to deal with trying to distinguish myself from the gypsies, people of Indian ethnicity who had migrated to Central and

Eastern Europe hundreds of years ago. The gypsies predominantly lived in impoverished and ghetto-like conditions. They were not looked upon very positively and were commonly discriminated against. I was regularly asked whether I was a gypsy, and when I said I was American, it totally confused them. I explained over and over that even though I was Indian-born, I was actually an American citizen, but eventually I gave up and just began telling people I was from India. The gypsies, thinking I was one of them, would speak to me in their language. They had a dialect of their own that resembled an Indic language mixed with Bulgarian.

Those days of sitting on the balcony pondering the interesting and often confusing nature of life are deeply embedded in my consciousness. Even though I had grown up as a Hindu, I had never very deeply pondered the questions of life. I do remember reflecting on the idea of reincarnation—wherein one accepts another body after death to continue one's sojourn in the material world—but because I had already gained and lost so much in such a short life, the idea of coming back to this world was quite unappealing. I was constantly asking myself, "Why is all of this happening to me?" After all, I wasn't a bad person. I hadn't hurt anyone so bad as to deserve all of this. I didn't really have any bad habits and had tried to live a fairly honest life. Why were life and destiny treating me this way?

It didn't seem like one would get rewarded for the good they had done. My father had tried to help people in his life. He was generous with his money and friendship, and in the opinion of my mom and myself, he was a bit too generous and trusting. That's the reason he had been cheated by people that worked for him or people he had partnered with. It felt like it didn't really matter whether one tried to help people or was callous towards them. Either way, bad things could happen.

It felt unfair. I wondered what role God played in all of this, if any. I couldn't help but compare my life now to the lives of all my friends in Los Angeles, and my family in India, who all seemed to be living "normal" lives—going to college, getting a job, and on their way to getting married and having a family.

THE BHAGAVAD GITA

Since most people in Bulgaria didn't speak or understand English at all, my dad had hired two secretaries who could help with the business and translate. One of them had learned English and could communicate fairly effectively, while the other could only speak and understand at a very basic level.

During her lunch breaks, I noticed her reading a book with a cover that looked familiar to one of the spiritual books I had had on my shelf in Los Angeles. I asked her where she had gotten such a book and what the content of it was, and she said someone at her college had given it to her. The book she was reading was the *Bhagavad Gita*. I was very fascinated by the text and its teachings and asked her to share with me what she was reading. She would try and explain to me whatever she could. Even though I don't remember what she told me, it was enough to make me obtain my own copy. So, when I visited Los Angeles for a short two weeks, I picked up a copy of the Gita to bring back to Bulgaria. I didn't have much else to do there; there were two channels on TV, one in Bulgarian and the other in Russian, and I had already seen the movies in the theaters. It was the perfect time to read.

I had made several attempts to read the *Bhagavad Gita* in the past, but it hadn't felt relevant. Life had been good, and I had never felt compelled to ask existential questions. This time, the *Gita* pierced me to the core of my soul. It spoke to me so powerfully that even on days that I worked from morning to night and felt exhausted, I still found time to read at least one verse. Mohandas Gandhi says:

> *When doubts haunt me, when disappointments stare me in the face, and I see not one ray of hope on the horizon, I turn to Bhagavad Gita and find a verse to comfort me; and I immediately begin to smile in the midst of overwhelming sorrow. Those who meditate on the Gita will derive fresh joy and new meanings from it every day.*

The *Bhagavad Gita*, which literally means "the Song of God," was spoken by Krishna, God incarnate, to His devotee and friend Arjuna at a time when Arjuna was at a major crossroads in his life. His father had passed away when he was still young; then, as a young man, his cousins and uncle betrayed him by cheating him and his four brothers out of a kingdom that was rightfully theirs.

After spending thirteen years in exile in the forest with his brothers and wife, he returned to request that his family's kingdom be restored to them, but was refused. Having no further recourse, Arjuna realized that in order for his family to survive, and to insure the welfare of the kingdom, he would have to wage war against his family members. His cousin had already made several attempts to murder Arjuna and his brothers and attempted to humiliate Arjuna's wife. When the day of battle arrived and both armies had assembled at Kurukshetra, a town in Northern India, Arjuna felt uncertain about his impending actions. He asked his charioteer, Krishna, to drive his chariot to the middle of the battlefield so he could see his opponents. When he saw his grandfather, who had raised him after his father's death, and his teacher, who had bestowed great affection on him, standing alongside his uncles and cousins ready to fight, Arjuna had a complete nervous breakdown.

His mind became clouded, and he no longer wanted to fight. His very bow was slipping from his hands. Ultimately, he sat down on his chariot in great grief, unable to lead the battle. At that crucial time, Arjuna turned to Krishna and asked him what should be done. Krishna was surprised by Arjuna's uncertainty. In his lifetime, Arjuna was one of the best warriors in the entire world. He was well known as confident, determined, and accomplished. He had always stuck to his decisions, and he had never backed down from a just cause.

My situation was definitely nowhere near as difficult as Arjuna's, but I did feel that I could relate to his frame of mind. Arjuna's situation was so extreme that it might seem unrelated to anyone's practical concerns and issues. However, just as Arjuna had to battle with his mind to make the right decisions, we all have our own battles that we're constantly going through. Most of us are fighting several battles simultaneously. Many high school students are faced with the stressful task of choosing a college and a new home for the next four years of their life. When they arrive at their new school, they might struggle with being away from their families and the comforts of home while learning to manage their own schedule. For some, there is the anxiety of attempting to choose a major and ultimately a career path. If you ask a college senior what they plan to do after graduating, most will tell you, "I'm still trying to figure it out." Finding someone you hope to spend the rest of your life with is a source of great worry as well. Even if you find "the one," there is so much anxiety about whether or not it's going to work out. After several relationships, figuring out how much energy to invest in a new relationship further complicates the issue. Marriage, kids, finances, retirement – who can say that these aren't battles? The *Bhagavad Gita* was spoken five-thousand years ago to Arjuna who was sitting on a chariot, but the advice Krishna offers in response to the problems of humanity are timeless.

It's possible that one needs to be in a certain frame of mind in order to grasp spiritual truths. Intellectually, we can comprehend spiritual knowledge, but without a crisis or real need for answers, the messages won't sink in to a point where they will change our lives. I was definitely ready to understand why all this happened, ready to know how to proceed in life with some kind of faith. The *Gita* gave me hope in life once again. It helped me to understand that there was a reason for everything, and that nothing was happening simply by random chance.

Within about six months, my dad had succeeded in importing a variety of clothing and jewelry from India and had established a business. For the first time in my life, I felt like a real adult—working, taking on responsibilities, and helping my father manage his business. I dealt with his clients and supplied them with merchandise. Later, I oversaw the retail store that he opened up. It was even enlivening at times. The future was still unclear, but I felt a sense of adventure about living in a different country, learning a new language, and taking on serious responsibilities.

After spending a year in Plovdiv, we moved to the capital, Sofia, seeking greater business opportunities. It turned out to be a good move, and our business expanded. It seemed there was some ray of hope for the future of our family. As difficult as that time was, it was probably my period of greatest learning.

For a good chunk of my life, I hadn't worked for anything and never had any responsibility. Because life was so simple, I had never felt motivated to accomplish or achieve anything. In Bulgaria, for the first time I felt a strong zeal to succeed. This was what I needed for a material and spiritual awakening to take place. Although it was a challenging time, it was what I needed to get up out of my slumber. In retrospect, I don't regret any of it. I learned things that I otherwise would not have learned.

LESSONS IN BULGARIA

While reading the Gita, one of the most pivotal tenets I learned was that everything in life was temporary. Up until coming to Bulgaria, I thought that after college I would take over my dad's business, get married, and lead my life like other people. In my wildest dreams, I couldn't have imagined what was going to happen to me. I related to a profound verse about this from the second chapter:

> *O son of Kuntī, the nonpermanent*
> *appearance of happiness and distress, and*
> *their disappearance in due course, are like the*
> *appearance and disappearance of winter and*
> *summer seasons. They arise from sense*
> *perception, O scion of Bharata, and one must*
> *learn to tolerate them without being*
> *disturbed.*

The theme of this verse is tolerance and acceptance. We know the seasons are changing. After summer passes, winter has to come. Even if we're not very fond of winter, we still have to prepare for it and tolerate it—we have no choice. The nature of happiness and distress are very much the same. No one wakes up hoping for distress, but it comes regardless of our own desires. We don't want our happiness to end, but inevitably, it does. On the other hand, happiness will also sometimes come unexpectedly. There's no stopping this cycle. The *Gita* suggests that we try our best to tolerate, accept, and maintain a steady mind during these cycles.

Reading this verse about the seasons helped me see the bigger picture of life and understand the state of mind I should aspire for. It's not that I was able to attain that state of mind, but I understood what my end goal should be when things got frustrating. The Gita also emphasizes that everything in the material world is temporary. Everything we acquire through our hard work will eventually diminish in quality and value. Gain and loss, victory and defeat are the dichotomies of the world of matter. All matter—clothes, cars, houses, gadgets, and even our bodies—must decay and eventually disappear. Even our relationships can lose their charm after some years. Ultimately, death will separate us from everything we own and love. When I first read these teachings, I felt like my eyes were opened for the first time in my life. I began to realize that there was more to life than trying to accumulate money and material success. Before I studied these teachings, I was deluded into believing that my world was permanent, and because of this I was devastated when I lost everything, including my friends.

There is a German proverb in that says, "The last coat you wear will have no pockets." We come into this world naked, and that's exactly how we will leave. Holding onto the temporary things of this world is like trying to hold water in one's hands. No matter how hard we try, it will all slip away. My parents had tried desperately to keep things intact, but everything fell away one after the other, and now here we were trying to gain it all back. The Gita had me questioning life and the purpose behind all of our actions, and I wasn't used to thinking this way.

The other concept that resonated with me at the time was *karma*. I was vaguely familiar with the idea that what you do comes back to you, but I had never really pondered it in much depth. The Gita explained that almost everything that happens in our lives is a product of our actions, either from this life or from previous lives. It's hard to trace why something is happening to us. I can't say this particular teaching of the Gita sat well with me at first. After all, it was basically telling me I was responsible for my current situation. It was more like a slap in the face than a source of comfort. I knew that in the present life, I had had a comfortable upbringing and hadn't caused harm to anyone else. I felt uneasy with the idea that I was possibly suffering for something I had done in a past life. I hadn't really accepted the idea of past lives, and certainly didn't know enough about karma to understand that it carries over to the next birth.

Indian people, including myself, like to joke in casual conversation about what they might have been in a previous life or what they might become in a future life, but I had never considered that my past life could influence my present one. As disconcerting as the concept was, I couldn't just ignore it. It was a tough pill to swallow, but it made me reflect on the concept of karma and reincarnation, and on why all these drastic changes were happening in my life.

The police in Bulgaria were quite unpredictable. On the highway, they could stop you without reason. If they thought you had money, they would stop you, waste your time until you slipped them some money, and then let you get on with your business.

The most frightening thing I remember about Bulgaria was in Sofia, when a police officer randomly pulled me over to see what was in my car. When I asked him, in my best Bulgarian possible, what I had done wrong, he pointed his gun at me and said, "I can shoot you right now." I had never been so scared in my life. I didn't know what to do; I couldn't know what his intentions were. I thought of running, but I stayed. He could have done anything, since law and order was quite topsy-turvy in the country at that time. After letting me sit around for a while, he told me I could go.

Oftentimes, I would travel between cities to deliver merchandise to our customers or collect money that was owed to us. All business transactions were in cash—no one wrote checks and credit cards didn't exist. I took our van or the train, and I often carried a briefcase full of Bulgarian money when I traveled. In dollars it wasn't that much, but for a local person, it was probably enough money to survive on for several months. We decided that it would be a good idea for me to carry pepper spray for protection; fortunately I never needed to use it. I don't know how effective it would have been. I was 22 years old and a little naïve, so I never fully realized the potentially dangerous nature of the work.

As the government in Bulgaria became increasingly unstable, corruption increased. The mafia had shown up to our retail store demanding money. Being foreigners was becoming riskier by the day, so we decided to return to the United States. We no longer felt safe walking around and doing our day-to-day activities.

After all that had happened, we didn't want to go back to Los Angeles. Instead, my parents decided to head to the East Coast. They chose Jersey City because of its proximity to Manhattan, and here they hoped to start a new life.

CHAPTER FOUR

MEDITATION, MORTGAGES, AND NEW JERSEY

I had mixed feelings about coming back to America. On the one hand, it was good to be in a country where I could communicate with people easily and have the technological facilities I was used to. On the other, this would be the third time that I was starting over, and I was only 23.

We didn't have any friends or family in the area. With the little money that we had earned in Bulgaria, my parents purchased a small two-bedroom house in Jersey City and a compact car. We would have to work hard to get the business up and running, and we didn't have a lot of savings. The only thing left from our previous fortune was some furniture and clothing, but we were grateful just to have a roof over our head and a car.

We managed to start a retail store in Midtown Manhattan that sold clothing and gift items from India. We had invested all we had left into the store, setting aside just a few months' worth of rent. It was an uphill battle. We had to compete with many similar retailers that were quite established. It became obvious within the first year that we weren't going to survive. Within two years we shut down, having exhausted most of whatever we had saved up.

It was a very difficult time for my parents. They were in their 50s with no savings, and my mom had to enter into retail work to bring in any additional money she could. I realized that I was going to have to get a job as well. My dad knew someone in the mortgage business and they agreed to hire me. In 1997, I worked my first official job and made $700 a month. I didn't have many choices about working, and tried to see this as an opportunity to learn a new trade. My dad stayed at home trying to figure out what his next move was going to be. With only two small incomes, we were barely getting by.

PARENTS

In retrospect, I can't even imagine what my father was going through or how he felt. He is a very smart and shrewd businessman, and has always lived a very active and dynamic life. His father was a very successful and influential politician during the British rule in India. Only two people in the town of Lucknow had a car, and my grandfather was one of them. However, he passed away when my father was only seven years old. His death forced my father to grow up really fast; he saw his family fortune looted by friends and family while his mother, a housewife, stood by helpless to do anything about it. He had to take care of himself, his mother, two younger brothers, and an older sister. He started working odd jobs when he was nine years old, and in time learned the ways of the world and how to understand people.

Many times he would sleep on the cold, hard floor on the banks of the river Ganges, and often he would pass days without food. He didn't have money to buy books for school, so he would borrow books from his friends, study under a street lamp, and pass the tests, oftentimes acing them. Unable to afford train tickets, he would sneak onto moving trains when he needed to travel to other towns. He would jump off when security spotted him, although sometimes the security did catch him and beat him. It was hard for him to understand how his life could have changed so quickly.

My dad met my mom while he was working as a tutor, one of his many jobs at the time. She was his student, and she fell in love. He didn't return her feelings initially—she was six years younger and only thirteen years old—but in time, she won him over. It was her simplicity that he came to adore. Her sensibilities are very different from my father's sense of extravagance: she can be happy in a small house with minor comforts as long as her family is close by. After discovering that she had a crush on him, he let her down gently. She responded by asking him, "what should I tell everyone?" This response melted his heart and he gradually developed affection for her.

Her family opposed the match because my dad was poor whereas my mom was from a wealthy background; the only way they could meet was secretly in the middle of the night on the rooftop, away from outside eyes. My dad would climb up three stories using a plumbing pipe that was attached to the side of the building. Their romance was innocent but dedicated.

On the day my mom finished college, my dad took her to a courthouse and married her. Eloping was not seen as romantic at the time in India, but rather a source of shame. My mother's father was so embarrassed that he didn't come out of his house for months.

My dad had an adventurous and risk-taking side, and he was always looking to do something big—something great. He never settled for anything small. This same risk-taking tendency is what led him to lose his fortunes so many times. Even though he's shrewd, he is quick to trust people who help him even a little bit. That trust has caused him to get cheated out of tons of money throughout his life. I can only suppose that since he had to take care of himself for so much of his life he gets a certain satisfaction in helping others, even if it's at the risk of taking away from his family.

Through thick and thin, and God only knows all that my mother and father went through, they stuck it out and remained together. I don't know how they pulled it off through so many struggles and so much moving. I am really grateful to them for always staying together; I can't imagine what would have happened to me emotionally if they hadn't.

Knowing the kind of life my dad had led made seeing him in this very uncertain state especially difficult for both my mom and myself. This was probably one of the first times in his life that he was dependent on another's income. Fortunately, I got better jobs in the mortgage industry, but even then, it wasn't enough to support a three-person family, a house, and a car. I had nothing left to myself at the end of the month.

The future seemed bleak. I often wondered how long would things continue in this way. How could I get married when I already had a couple of people to support and no savings in the bank? I was so busy working that there was no time or opportunity to try to meet anyone.

THE MORTGAGE BUSINESS

The mortgage business was a brutal, high-pressure industry. Employees would come and go, and I worked at four companies within a two-year period. We were given a monthly salary, but we were required to sell a certain number of loans each month. This meant convincing people to take loans that would only provide short-term benefits, even though they were already drowning in debt. I knew that these people shouldn't have been given loans in the first place.

They had maxed out their credit cards on clothing, appliances, cars, and other inessentials—now they wanted to mortgage their homes to pay off their debts. It was toxic. My job was paying our bills, but it certainly wasn't helping people. On the contrary, I was convincing people that they were helping themselves, when they were actually risking the very roof they lived under. It was quite sad and it weighed heavily on my conscience, but I felt trapped by my situation. A majority of the household responsibility fell on my shoulders.

When I had first joined the mortgage industry, it all seemed kind of exciting. It was my first real job and my first opportunity to do something on my own. At my second company, I got to witness corporate politics in action. After I had trained most of the staff, a new employee, who was related to the regional manager, got promoted to assistant manager. Not seeing a future for myself at this company, I looked for different opportunities.

The third bank provided a much better salary and commission structure. However, the boss at the new place was intense and mean. She had an amazing memory—so amazing, in fact, that she remembered everything about you and reminded you of it with ruthless efficiency. She was being pressured by her bosses to produce results and that results-oriented environment brought out the worst in her. My motivation decreased as I felt more and more out of touch with what I wanted out of life. Many of the people I had initially worked with at the company had quit as the work increased and the pay decreased.

One of my coworkers at that company was a heavy-set Italian guy who sat at the desk in front of me, and he was a smooth-talker. Part of the job was making cold calls to customers, and part of it was receiving loan requests as a result of mailers the company would send out. He constantly flirted with female clientele. During the application process, we would get to know a lot about the client and he would use that information to try to meet up with the women that would call in. I don't know if he actually succeeded, but sometimes he would tell me that he had met up with some of them and scored. I wasn't sure if I believed him or not. The mortgage business was a revolving door; I saw many people come and go.

I jumped ship once again. In early 1998, my second year in the mortgage industry, I returned to the initial push toward spirituality that I had adopted in Bulgaria—vegetarianism, meditation, and reading the *Bhagavad Gita*. All of this had fallen by the wayside after we came back to the U.S, but being frustrated with life, I again found myself in need of the same spiritual shelter that I had sought in Bulgaria. It was the only thing that could give me peace of mind and something greater to live and hope for.

I became quite serious in my spiritual pursuits. I re-adopted the vegetarian diet prescribed by the bhakti tradition of Hinduism, which meant avoiding all types of meats, fish, and eggs. Milk wasn't banned because it doesn't have the potential for life as eggs do. It wasn't easy. I realized I had become addicted to the taste of meat, and it took me a whole year to leave behind my carnivorous cravings.

One of the principle teachings of Hinduism is Ahimsa, or non-violence. It emphasizes the need to recognize life in all species and to respect that life as much as we would respect human life. In order for us to develop love of God, the essential goal of Hinduism, we must develop a compassionate heart, which means not interfering with the life of other living beings— birds, animals, fish, etc.

Why should we unnecessarily cause or contribute to the physical or mental suffering of others? Animals run in fear and try to protect their own lives as much as we would. They defend the lives of their families and children just like any human would. There is enough suffering in the world, so we can do our part in reducing it by not harming other species whether they are two-legged, four-legged, the winged, or the gilled.

People argue that "killing plants is also killing," and I agree with that. Violence in this world cannot be obliterated, but we can do our best to minimize it. Most fruits will fall off the tree when ripe and many plants will regrow the vegetables after being harvested. Moreover, fruits and vegetables don't have a central nervous system, so they don't feel pain in the same way humans and animals do.

On the weekends, I started frequenting the local temples in Manhattan and Brooklyn, where I sat in on the philosophical discourses. I was actively studying the *Bhagavad Gita* and the *Puranas,* ancient historical accounts of kings and sages who taught by example. During my lunch breaks at work, I would eat in my car while listening to recorded lectures delivered by senior monks. It was my only solace in life, the only thing that seemed to make sense.

After several visits to the temple, I finally mustered up the courage to talk to one of the monks after his lecture. He agreed and we went downstairs for dinner and talked for at least an hour. After studying the Gita independently for so long, I was full of questions, and he took time to carefully answer all of them. I asked him about karma, the purpose of life, how we got here, why God had created us in the first place. He listened patiently and responded as best he could.

As I continued to visit the temples, my hunger for spiritual knowledge only increased, filling a void that I had always felt. Our sessions would go later and later into the night every Sunday. I would continue to meet the same monk because our conversations always left me hopeful and excited about life, a feeling I hadn't had in the eight years since I left Los Angeles.

I began to regularly practice mantra meditation, a central tenet of the spiritual texts that I was reading and the lectures that I was listening to. I started with ten minutes a day and gradually increased to two hours over a one-year period, while maintaining a full-time job. I couldn't explain to myself why I was pursuing my spirituality so aggressively. All I knew was that it was giving me a deeper and more satisfying experience than I'd ever had.

My parents worried about my passionate spiritual pursuits. It's quite natural for Indian parents to worry if their son or daughter gets too religious, especially if they aren't married. The Hindu scriptures place a certain amount of emphasis on renunciation of the material. This renunciation isn't just for monks; all are encouraged to practice a certain amount of detachment. However, because many of the tradition's teachers over the last 5,000 years have been monks who started pursuing spirituality early in life and who left behind their families in pursuit of truth, Hindu parents worry their children might renounce material life and take to the monastic order, instead of becoming a doctor or an engineer. Of course, the biggest fear Hindu parents have is being bereft of grandchildren, and therefore not being able to continue on the family name. I think the other reason my mom was worried was because her mother, while in her 30s, left behind five kids to live in a monastery for women. It seemed like this kind of thing ran in the family. Of course, my grandfather brought her back home.

However, they never discouraged me from the choices I was making. They saw that after many years I was finally experiencing some contentment in life and that I was becoming a nicer person. They even visited the temple with me a few times just to check things out.

I was losing all motivation at work. It had become meaningless. Since I had already witnessed the addictive and fleeting nature of money, it just didn't seem important anymore. Selling loans from an office cubicle wasn't something I could see myself doing for the rest of my life, or for even another few months. It began to feel like every hour lasted an eternity. Driving to work was dreadful. Once there, I looked forward to my lunch hour and six o'clock when I could leave. Even as my motivation for money and success declined, I continued to feel the weight of our household affairs on my shoulders. I had no choice but to drag myself to and from work everyday.

I found myself asking when this would all come to an end. After all, life just couldn't go on like this, could it? Feeling trapped and even depressed, I found solace in my newfound spirituality that I didn't find anywhere else in life.

SPIRITUAL APPROACH TO SUFFERING

In the seventh chapter of the *Bhagavad Gita,* Krishna explains that there are four types of people who approach Him: those who are distressed, those seeking money, the inquisitive, and the wise. I was one of the distressed.

Hindu scriptures explain that suffering comes from three sources. The first is the suffering that arises from material nature, in the form of bad weather or natural disasters—hurricanes, earthquakes, tornadoes, etc. The second type of suffering is caused by other living beings, including insects, animals, or other human beings that may bring upon us physical, financial, and/or emotional distress. The final category of suffering comes from our own bodies and minds. Diseases, aches and pains, cuts and bruises or other injuries are suffering that result from the body. The mind is always harboring many stresses. Hindu texts explain that the mind is the ultimate source of suffering for the human being. Only a healthy mind can assist us when dealing with distressing and painful situations.

It's usually when something breaks down that we actually look for a solution. The problem with this approach is that when something breaks, we are caught off guard. We tend to use spirituality like medicine or a hospital; we utilize it only when things aren't going right or when we're suffering financially, emotionally, or relationally. Our pain and suffering, however, can be a path to transcending a selfish conception of spirituality into something more. We reach out to God and expect Him to keep things as they are or fix them and make everything all right. This need-based spirituality is superficial and should be transcended.

That is the frame of mind Arjuna was in when he began to inquire from Krishna about his duty and purpose in life. Arjuna's mother, Kunti, makes a similar statement about the time of struggle being the most fertile time for spiritual growth. While praying to Krishna, she says that only those who are "materially exhausted" can approach Him with sincere feelings, while those who possess wealth, beauty, and fame may struggle to pray with depth and realization. She is not making an absolute statement that the wealthy are unable to make sincere inquiries about the goal of life, but rather that they are commonly distracted by all these facilities. She further admits that the challenges and suffering she experienced in her own life have helped her in her spiritual pursuits by compelling her to learn to take shelter in something divine, and not just in her material facilities.

Many spiritual teachers from the Hindu tradition encourage us to welcome suffering into our lives and allow it to give us the necessary wakeup call that we might otherwise ignore. Difficulties teach us patience, tolerance, acceptance, and ultimately that we're not in complete control of our lives. We can do everything perfectly and things might still not go our way. Some of the greatest teachers within Hinduism demonstrated by example that our soul can experience the greatest spiritual growth during challenging times; they also demonstrated that we can actually thank God for the difficulty. In the ancient histories known as the *Purana*, a devotee offers the following prayer:

> *My dear Lord, one who earnestly waits for*
> *You to bestow Your causeless mercy upon*

*him, all the while patiently suffering the
reactions of his past misdeeds and offering
You respectful obeisances with his heart,
words and body, is surely eligible for
liberation, for it has become his rightful claim.*

In this verse, the devotee isn't even turning toward God to mitigate his suffering. Rather, he is accepting whatever is coming as his own karma while simultaneously offering full respects to God. The devotee isn't blaming God, nor asking anything from Him. The concluding line of this verse suggests that a practitioner of this consciousness is already liberated because he or she is free from blame and lamentation.

Suffering can be a state of mind. How much we suffer from a situation, in one sense, really depends on us, but no matter how much we try to avoid it, it's going to make its way into our lives. Knowing this, we should live our lives so that we're able to grow from it.

Life had brought me to a state of mind where I was ready to try something different, even something drastic. By the time I was 27, I had experienced a lot of different things in my life and none of them had ever satisfied me. People always ask me what made me become a monk, and I know they're looking for a quick answer. Even after living as a monk for so many years, I'm still usually speechless, struggling to provide an answer that will be relatable and understandable. I have realized that there isn't a short answer to such a question. I've learned to provide one-liners to satisfy people because often this is what they want, but to truly understand my decision would be as difficult as understanding why anyone behaves a certain way. When giving the short answer, I say, "I was looking for something deeper in life than making money and acquiring possession, so I wanted to take some time and explore that."

If they have more time, I offer deeper explanation. It's not as if I woke up one day and decided to renounce the world and all that it has to offer. If you ask a child what he or she'd like to become, the standard answer is doctor, lawyer, teacher, astronaut, firefighter, etc. These vocations are glorified by the public and are seen as substantial contributions to society. The image people have of monks is that they're removed from the world to focus on their own spiritual lives. When was the last time a child told someone that they wanted to become a monk or nun? For the most part, it's not something you know at an early age. Even when I was in the process of becoming a monk, I didn't know that this was the lifestyle I'd end up living for an extended period of time. Practically all of the monks I've come across in my sojourn had no inclination towards this lifestyle until they were in college or working or until they came across another monk. It's usually not something you plan for. Life will bring you to that point.

CHAPTER FIVE

THE MONKS OF MUMBAI

I knew something had to change, but I had no clue what I should do. Our family's financial situation was still very precarious. We had still not recovered from the collapse of our family fortunes in Los Angeles. One day, as I was sitting in the New York temple, looking up at the altar in a mood of desperation, I prayed for something to happen, and something did. The temple president announced that a trip was being organized for those interested in going to visit some of the holy places of India. Right then and there, I knew instantly this is what I had to do. I had to go to India! I desperately wanted to get away from my job, the depressing situation at my home, and the intensely materialistic environment of America. Deep down inside, I knew this was the answer and I had to follow this calling.

I felt as if God had heard my prayers and was giving me the much-needed direction I'd been looking for. Not too long after that, my father succeeded in some of his business deals and was able to maintain the household affairs on his own. I knew at this time that I could quit my job if I wanted to and perhaps go to India. But seeing my father's business succeed, I was tempted to join him and treat myself right for a change. After all, I had experienced pretty serious financial and emotional hardships for almost eight years since I had left Los Angeles. There was a voice within me saying that this was the small window that had opened up to pursue my spiritual life, and that if I didn't jump through that window and go to India that window might close and not open up again. I kept remembering how everything I had owned had been stripped away from me by the forces of time and karma, and how my possessions had never really satisfied me in the first place. Did I once again want to try to enjoy something temporary and material?

The decision to go to India wasn't as easy as I had thought it would be. The thought of living in a communal setting made me anxious. I'm an only child and have always had my own room, TV, stereo, bathroom, car, and parking space. I never really had to share anything with anyone and had always been able to do what I wanted, when I wanted, and how I wanted. This was definitely something I had to seriously consider. But there wasn't much else holding me back; my parents were supportive and didn't raise any emotional roadblocks. Internally, I can't say I knew what they were going through, but I knew I had to go, no matter what.

THE TEMPLE AND MONASTERY IN MUMBAI

A couple of the monks in New York had suggested a monastery in Mumbai. Someone from the Mumbai temple's congregation happened to be visiting New York. He wasn't a monk but a software engineer. He was here for a work project and we got to know each other. I started inquiring about the temple and monastic life. He had been part of the Mumbai community for many years and had even spent many a night in this particular monastery.

The monastery sat smack in the middle of a very busy section of Mumbai. It was only a block away from the ocean and was surrounded by apartment complexes and shops selling fruits, vegetables, flowers, and other household goods. Once in a while, cows walked by, and cars, scooters, three-wheeled rickshaws, and taxis noisily raced around on the nearby streets. The front door gave way to a large courtyard which led to the two-story, dilapidated building which housed the temple on the second floor, a school for kids, and a small internet café. Not exactly what you imagine when you think of a monastery.

He told me how austere the lifestyle was, explaining how everyone slept on the wooden floor, just a few feet apart, on thin straw mats, and that everyone used mosquito nets to not get bitten and come down with malaria. Sometimes the monks would come back late at night from some kind of outreach program, so the monastery wasn't a very quiet place to sleep. No matter how late someone returned, they had to be up by 4am because the morning services started at 5am sharp. If anyone was late, they would be required to do extra services in the temple. There were about forty monks living in the monastery, and there was a line in the morning to use the bathroom, as everyone was required to brush their teeth and shower before entering the temple room. There were no laundry machines, so all clothes had to be hand-washed. He also told me the food was quite simple, but freshly cooked and everybody sat and ate together. He also warned me, if one person got sick, then many others also fell ill because they all live so closely together.

Convinced that no matter how challenging and difficult this all sounded, I was determined to give my spiritual life a serious try. I needed to dive in without any distractions, so I quit my job; knowing that I didn't have to go to work the next day was a liberating experience. One of the monks from New York wrote a letter to the temple in Mumbai informing them of my visit and requesting permission for a one-month stay in their temple. Very quickly, we received an approval for my stay.

I purchased my ticket and had a month before I was to leave. I spent that month getting mentally prepared for the trip and the new lifestyle. I spent extra time at the local temple doing service, reading scriptures, memorizing prayers, and telling the different members of the community about my decision. The month passed by pretty quickly and before I knew it, the day had arrived and I was ready to go. My parents didn't know the way to the airport, so they dropped me off at Grand Central station on 42nd street and from there I took a bus to John F. Kennedy International airport. I had a suitcase and a backpack and was planning to be in India for about a month.

After an almost 24 hour, door-to-door trip, I landed in Mumbai. It was an overnight flight and I arrived at the temple around seven in the morning, still dizzy from the journey. I settled in, showered and entered the temple hall. As I walked into the temple, the morning lecture was just beginning. I put away my belongings and the next phase of my life was about to begin.

It's important to remember that my plan was to just visit India for about a month and then go back and continue life where I had left it, which meant either looking for a different job or working with my father. I didn't come to India with the idea of becoming a monk. Rather, it was supposed to be a time of reflection and clarity. I had no idea that this would turn into a life-changing experience.

Since I wasn't used to waking so early, I was really worried about not being able to get up on time. I sure didn't want the New York temple and the monk who wrote the letter of recommendation for me to look bad. I went to bed at 8:00 PM, figuring that if I got enough sleep, I should be able to wake up on time. They had put me into this tiny room, and I shared it with a few other Western monks who were visiting from different parts of the world. It turns out that that was the room given to all visiting monks. It was quite crowded and our suitcases and clothing were all over the place on the floor.

There were no closets for visitors, so we were all living out of our suitcases. One of the monks I met there had been living in a monastery in San Jose California; a few years later, we would end up living together in the same monastery in New York. He was there to film a documentary on the temple. I remember getting up at 4:00 a.m., grabbing my towel and heading towards the communal bathrooms. I had heard that the monastery didn't use toilet paper, so I had brought my own. When I approached the bathroom area, I saw lines in front of the sink, the showers, and the toilets. I had hid the toilet paper because I didn't want to look like the odd one out.

I had no soap, so I asked one of the monks if I could borrow some and he kindly gave me his. Later, when I went to return the soap to the monk, I couldn't find him. It was quite a busy scene as monks were running to and from the bathroom, placing the sacred markings on their bodies, and putting on their robes. In all truth, I couldn't recognize which monk had given me the soap. They all had shaved heads and robes, so I couldn't really tell them apart.

Putting on the robes to attend the morning service wasn't an easy task. These aren't simple robes you just throw on like a gown. It's called a dhoti. There's a whole elaborate system of pleating them and wrapping them around, pulling them between your legs, and tucking them in towards the back. The cloth is around eight to twelve feet in length and about four to five feet in height. It took me almost 15 minutes to put it on. I had only worn it a couple of times before while in New York so I had little experience of it. Then I had to place the sacred markings, or *tilak*. The *tilak* is formed from hardened clay-like substances obtained from the different holy places in India. They consist of two vertical lines going from in between the eyebrows to the top of the forehead. The bottom portion of these lines meet to form a "u" shape. These lines represent the footprint of God, indicating that we are placing God's feet on our head. On the upper portion of the nose, there's an arrow-like design pointing downward. This represents the leaf of the Tulsi plant, which is very dear to Krishna. Finally, I was ready to go, excited about attending my first morning ceremony with the monks. The four hour ceremony was a combination of lively singing and dancing, done for the pleasure of God, followed by a mantra meditation session which lasted almost two hours, and a lecture by one of the monks which went for about an hour.

Breakfast was served at 9:00 a.m. We all went eagerly towards the cafeteria, and there was a certain excitement as the monks came together for their first meal of the day. Breakfast was quite simple yet tasty fare—usually hot milk and some flat rice. Everyone had their own round stainless steel plate with three compartments and a stainless steel cup, all with the individual monk's initials. In a communal setting, it can be really easy to lose your belongings, which were few.

At the dining hall, mats were laid out on the floor and everyone would sit in long rows while some of the monks would serve. Most of the monks ate with their hands, which is the way people have always eaten in India. The British introduced eating utensils. I was a bit familiar with this custom already, because whenever my mom would cook chapattis or parathas (Indian flat breads), we would eat this way. The Hindu tradition explains that eating with your hands allows one to feel more in touch with the food. It felt like I was reconnecting with my Indian roots and realized I was enjoying the experience.

I was already feeling happy to be living a life of simplicity, away from all the sophistication of modern life. Three days had gone by and I hadn't left the temple complex; I don't think I'd ever been in one place for three days without going outside. In all honesty, I hadn't known if I'd even last for three days with this lifestyle, but by that point, I remember feeling very at ease and peaceful and probably more satisfied than I'd ever felt.

I felt that something profound was happening. I can't explain what, but there was a deep feeling of contentment. The monks were all very kind and eager to serve one another, and this was an environment very different from that of the West where everyone seemed to be out for him or herself.

I felt a certain gratitude to my parents for only speaking Hindi at home, because although most of the monks were highly educated and fluent in English, a lot of times they would go back and forth from English to Hindi. Being able to understand the monks and communicate in Hindi helped me to go a bit deeper in my relationships with them. Even though my Hindi was quite undeveloped, as I had only used Hindi to communicate with my parents and had all western friends growing up, I knew enough to get by. Some of the other visiting Western monks would at times feel a bit alienated because they couldn't understand the language. There were a wide variety of men from all parts of the world – Ukraine, Russia, England, and America. They were always treated with the utmost respect and helped in every way, but the language barrier made it more challenging for them to develop deep relationships with the local Indian monks. This became especially apparent right before bedtime, when many monks would huddle together and talk about the day's activities or discuss personal things. Because these conversations were in local languages, the visiting monks would either talk amongst themselves, read a book, or listen to devotional music on their headphones. I was fortunate to be able to be a part of these huddles, as I could understand most of everything that was being said. It didn't take too long to start forming relationships with the other monks, who were all very kind. Some of the monks really liked my "American" accent and would try and imitate it, without much success.

Some of the monks were fascinated by the American lifestyle and knew a lot about the American pop culture, and one monk in particular would always ask me about it. I wasn't interested in answering his questions because I had had my fill and didn't really want to be reminded of what I had left behind, at least for now. I was trying to distance myself from the American culture, but almost every time he saw me he would ask whether I ever listened to different types of American music. I would answer quickly and hope to change the subject.

In about two weeks' time, I was fairly plugged into the schedule. I was responsible for sweeping and mopping part of the monastery and during lunch would either help out in the kitchen or serve the food. All of the monks, no matter how senior they were, were required to do menial services such as cleaning the floors and the bathrooms, helping to cook and serve meals, and doing their own laundry.

Since most of the monks were well educated and were able to learn the philosophy fairly quickly, they would lecture in universities, in people's homes and at large public events. Receiving this type of respect and adoration from the public can lead to the buildup of pride, which can curtail one's spiritual progress. To balance things out, it was required that all the monks engage in simple and humble services to help them develop a humble character. The thing that really surprised me, because it went totally against the way I was raised, was when I saw the most senior monk, who was also one of the temple presidents, on his hands and knees at 4:30 in the morning, cleaning the temple room floor before the morning services. In the outside world, the most senior people are those telling everyone else what to do, but the culture of this temple is that one needs to lead not just by giving orders, but by one's own example. I was deeply impressed.

Not only were the monks being trained in this culture of humility, but the congregation of married practitioners was also encouraged to follow these same principles. One day, after the Sunday service, which was attended by a little over 1,000 people from the local area, one of the monks came up to me and pointed to a person sitting humbly on the floor at the back of the temple room. He told me that he was one of the biggest industrialists in all of India.

I was really blown away. People of that kind of prominence usually want some special attention, but this fellow was just sitting in the crowd with everyone else with no special consideration. I had never seen a culture of humility like this before, and I was beginning to understand why several monks had recommended that I come to this particular temple, and why it had achieved the reputation it had. The idea was that no matter what position one had achieved in the world, while in the temple, everyone should see themselves as the servant of everyone else. Even in one's normal dealings with family, friends, and coworkers, one shouldn't feel superior to others in a way that is condescending to others or in an exploitative manner. No one should feel or act superior to anyone else. This mood permeated the entire temple atmosphere, and was like nothing I had ever seen or experienced before.

In the West, humility is usually seen as a weakness. The perception is that humble people get pushed around and don't really get anywhere in life, and one gets ahead by being competitive and aggressive. For the first time, I was able to witness the culture of humility and I desired to develop it. Humility and tolerance are key components of the Hindu tradition. Gandhi helped to free India through the virtues of humility and tolerance. Martin Luther King, Jr., who was inspired by Gandhi, also pushed forward the civil rights movement on the same principles. These two great figures demonstrate with their own examples the true power of humility and tolerance.

Shri Chaitanya, a fifteenth century saint of the Bhakti tradition, encouraged his followers to "*become more humble than a blade of grass, more tolerant than a tree, to offer all respects to others, and to expect none in return.*" His successors have elaborated on the meaning of this passage. A blade of grass is stepped on, but without complaining it continues to offer comfort to the individual. A tree stands tolerating the winter and summer seasons while continuing to offer all that it has to anyone and everyone. One pursuing spiritual truths is encouraged to become "more" tolerant than the tree. We live in "an eye for an eye" culture where dishonor and disrespect are not tolerated. The more materialistic a society becomes, the more these qualities of tolerance and forgiveness lose their prominence.

The Hindu texts are full of stories of individuals who forgave their persecutors. One such example is that of Draupadi, the wife of Arjuna, whose five sons were murdered in their sleep by someone who was very envious of her husband. When Arjuna captured the murderer and brought him before his lamenting wife and asked whether he should kill this criminal, she said, "I don't want his mother to suffer the way I'm suffering, so he should be freed." Another beautiful example of forgiveness is that of King Parikchit, who was cursed by Sringi, the son of a powerful sage, to die in seven days. The king didn't retaliate by counter-cursing or arresting the culprit. Rather, he just accepted it as his destiny and he decided to dedicate the remaining seven days of his life to purely spiritual pursuits. He put it beside him and moved on.

Jesus teaches the same virtue by example. While he was being crucified on the cross, he forgave his persecutor and prayed to God, saying, "Father, forgive them, for they do not know what they do." (Luke 23:34) In the book of Matthew 18:22, Peter asks Jesus how many times he should forgive his brother or sister who have sinned against him, up to seven times? Jesus responds, "I tell you, not seven times, but seventy-seven times." These and many other examples may seem out of reach to us and perhaps they are. Oftentimes, we can lose our cool if someone even looks at us the wrong way or gets in the way of our getting what we want or what we think we need. The term "road rage" is a perfect description of the direction our society is moving towards. People end up in fistfights, try to drive each other off the road, or in extreme situations try to kill each other because they got cut off while driving.

This shouldn't stop us from taking inspiration from the character and behavior of saintly individuals. Even if we're not able to attain the level of tolerance described in the lives of these great persons, if we can understand deep down that this is the right direction to move in, we should begin to take baby steps to move to the next level of tolerant behavior.

The last portion of the passage by Shri Chaitanya deals with the task of offering all respects to others and expecting none in return. This one seems equally difficult to comprehend. After all, what's wrong with wanting a little respect? If I have done something noteworthy, why shouldn't I let people know about it? The point being made by Chaitanya is that praise and respect can bolster the ego, making the work of self-realization much more difficult. It also forces us to analyze the reasons and motivations behind the things we do in life. Are we working only because we enjoy the recognition or are we working because we enjoy the work? Perhaps it's a combination of both. If no one recognized the work we're doing, would we still be able to perform at the same level? Would we get depressed if someone didn't pat us on the back or congratulate us for our accomplishment?

The wisdom of Chaitanya is promoting the concept of selfless service. For the most part, it's natural to expect some kind of reciprocation or award after we render service to another individual or a cause. This part of the passage encourages us to do it from the goodness of the heart and be satisfied that we had the chance to offer some service to another. Sometimes recognition and reward may come and at other times they may not. That should not be our concern. Rather, we should accept selfless service as it will elevate our consciousness.

The opposite of humility is pride. Pride makes us feel superior to others. It makes one think that they are in control of their life and the things around them. However, without developing a humble character, one can't really know God. If we feel that we know everything or that we can figure everything out empirically, then the doors that reveal spiritual truths will remain closed to us.

I continued to spend more time befriending many of the different monks. The great thing was that a lot of them were around my age. They were definitely fascinated with my decision to leave America and come to India to practice this lifestyle. Many individuals from different parts of the world had come to their monastery for some monastic training, but the monastery hadn't had an Indian-American come back to India for this purpose. Generally, when an Indian family goes to America, material prosperity is on top of the priority list. Similarly, I was fascinated by all of their stories. They were all so qualified and competent, and could easily be making more than decent money working in the world.

Several of the monks were from the prestigious Indian Institute of Technology (IIT), which is the most prominent engineering college in all of India. Graduates from this institution get recruited by American engineering firms right out of college and get paid very good salaries. I was fascinated to see these individuals living such simple and humble lives, giving up the possibility of a very successful material career. Surely there was something wonderful about their environment that was allowing them to forgo the pleasures of the world and share bathrooms with forty others. The more time I spent with them, I could see that they were very satisfied and happy. This is something I hadn't experienced in the last ten years and this is exactly what I wanted. At that time, I still wanted to go back to America and either get a job or work with my father and figure out some marriage plans, but the more time I spent with these blissful monks, the more their happiness rubbed off on me.

I was in some small way starting to feel happy again—happy with the simple life and happy with the friendships. I did feel a bit of an inferiority complex around all of them because they had engineering, medical, or business degrees. Some even had completed their graduate studies. They were incredibly learned in the scriptures and many had memorized entire sections of the *Bhagavad Gita* and some had the entire *Gita* memorized. Moreover, a lot of them were great singers and accomplished at playing the traditional instruments. I, on the other hand, was never all that studious and was musically pretty inept. In high school, I managed to earn a high enough GPA to get on the honor roll, but I think that was more because most of my friends were doing really well and I wanted to fit in.

I sure felt humbled around these monks. The amazing thing was that they never came across as being so qualified and talented. They were quite simple and modest in the way they carried themselves. It wasn't until you got to know them personally that you discovered how materially qualified they actually were and that many of them came from wealthy families. This was their training.

One monk that I felt especially comfortable with was also one of the temple's presidents. He was short in stature but very confident, full of energy, and had great enthusiasm about everything he did. He possessed such a youthful spirit, and was loved by everyone. It was a very interesting combination of attributes that I had never come across before in a person, and we connected well right from the beginning. His name was Keshava, and his story was a little different than the rest of the monks in the monastery. Unlike most of the monks, he had grown up in a small village a few hours from Mumbai and was one of the very few that didn't have a college degree. In 1987, at the age of eighteen, he had run away from home to live in the monastery. When I met him, he had already been living there for about thirteen years. He lectured powerfully on the scriptures and had earned the respect from the monks and the congregation on the merit of his integrity of character and knowledge of scripture.

I felt him to be like the big brother I never had—a spiritual big brother. While I was in the Mumbai monastery, he would try to pay a little extra attention to me. He did this with many of the foreign visitors because he knew they might feel isolated from the rest of the residents. He also encouraged other monks to come forward to talk to me and befriend me. Whether it was questions about the philosophy, the practices, monastic life, or the history of the temple and tradition, he would make himself available to provide answers that always satisfied my curiosity and intellect. In fact, over the years we continue to stay in touch, over phone, email, or Skype, and keep each other updated on the events and changes that are taking place in our lives.

Another senior monk, who shared the role of temple president, very humorously asked me if I knew what the term "ABCD" stood for. Being a bit confused by his question, I professed my ignorance. With a big smile on his face, he said "American Born Confused Desi." "Desi" refers to one who is of Asian-Indian origin. I could only smile and see how easily he had realized that this was very much my situation. This is the term Indians in India use to describe their American counterparts. It really is a very good description because a lot of Indian-American kids struggle with their identity. To balance things out, Indian-American and other Asian communities have a term known as "FOB" which stands for "Fresh Off the Boat." Of course, this term refers to those Indians and other Asians who arrive in America after spending their youth and part of their adult life in India or Asia. They speak with an Indian accent, dress a little different, and their mannerisms are quite distinct from those raised in America. My Filipino friends used to refer to their family members who were raised in the Philippines and had come over to the U.S. in their young adulthood as "fobs."

A month or so into my stay, I felt inspired to shave or at least "buzz" my hair. The monks told me that in order for me to do that I would need to get permission. Generally, having a completely shaved head is the sign of one who has gone beyond the "figuring out stage" and has accepted the monastic lifestyle for at least some period of time. It's not meant to be taken cheaply or as a fad. I approached the same monk who had introduced me to the term "ABCD." Since he was also a temple president I asked if I could buzz my hair. Seeing my eagerness, he consented. I wasn't completely shaving my head, so it wasn't such a big deal. I was still a guest, so the rules weren't yet as stringent for me as they were for the permanent residents.

Soon, I began accompanying some of the monks into the local colleges to assist them with their college outreach programs. Some students on campus would organize talks and invite the monks to come and lecture or lead meditation sessions. Usually, a team of two monks would travel by train to the university, deliver a lecture and serve a vegetarian meal and then meet one-on-one with the students and answer questions. I found this to be very appealing and really enjoyed going to the colleges with them. I was so impressed with their ability to deliver relevant and thought-provoking talks to the college students and simultaneously befriend them. The students were so grateful that the monks would make the hour-long trek on local trains with freshly cooked food and render this service of not only enlightening them with knowledge, but also feeding them.

Riding the local Bombay trains is an almost indescribable experience, in contrast to the serenity we had been cultivating as monks. Bombay trains make

New York subway cars feel like business class. There's no air conditioning, just some fans that blow warm air in the perpetual hot and muggy climate of Mumbai. Each train compartment is packed with people holding three times its capacity. As the train pulls into the station, a dozen people hang out of the train ready to jump out onto the platform. The trains don't have doors. Simultaneously, people on the platform start running to board the train. At times it can look like two opposing armies clashing on a battlefield. For the local people, it's just another day taking the train, but to me it looked insanely dangerous. Getting on and off are the scary parts. As the crowd starts to exit, you had better get out of the exit aisle, otherwise the crowd will take you with them whether it is your stop or not. Once you actually get on the train, you're pretty much going to stay wherever you are because you're just packed in there like a herd of animals. On a couple of occasions, I nearly lost my flip-flops and was close to getting my glasses smashed by the crowds.

I definitely wouldn't recommend riding the trains alone, and to this day I try my very best to avoid the local trains at rush hour. But it's not like taking a taxi is that much better. The traffic is horrendous and most of the taxis don't have any air conditioning or smog protection so each car blows black smoke, which is hard to avoid. So, either it's getting stampeded by the crowds on the trains and at the stations or inhaling a ton of carbon monoxide. In recent years, cabs in Bombay are being equipped with newer cars that have air conditioning and a smoother ride. I can confidently say that every experience in India, whether it's traveling, eating, shopping or whatever else, will be very unique and different than in the West.

Many of the regular congregation members would also invite the monks to their homes for a discourse to their friends and relatives. The congregation was a cross-section of Indian society—young, old, housewives, businessmen, students, doctors, engineers, lawyers, and people of all walks of life. Before starting the talk, the monks would introduce me as someone who had grown up in America and come to India to explore spiritual life. They would emphasize my coming from America to such a degree that it became embarrassing. They made me look like I was some kind of savior that had left the land of materialism behind and come to save them. This was really awkward, because I was a mere novice and knew little or nothing about the tradition. I could barely get my robes on. America is portrayed as the land of dreams where all of ones aspirations can be fulfilled. If America had everything, then why would I be coming to India? They were trying to communicate the idea that the grass isn't greener on the other side. I realized it was an attempt to discourage them from coming to America and getting lost in materialism. Divorce statistics and drugs usage amongst the youth and adults were often given as examples of the downside of Western culture to balance out the image of the

American dream people had in their minds from television shows. Sometimes, the quoting of such statistics would bother me because America had become my home and had given my family great opportunities. But one of the reasons my parents left India was because of the corruption. Every country and every part of the world has its amazing qualities and its deficiencies. America and India are no exceptions.

Sometimes the monks would even ask me to speak a few words, but I didn't like public speaking and wasn't good at it, so I would politely refuse. I didn't really know the philosophy well enough to speak about it. Mostly, they would just want me to talk about my experiences in America and what it was that made me want to come to India. I think the thing they found fascinating was that I was born in India, grew up in America, and then came back to India to rediscover myself. In addition to living a contemplative life incorporating the study of scriptures, the monks were encouraged to utilize their talents and creativity in presenting spirituality to others in a way that would be interesting and relevant. The understanding was "in giving we receive," and that by helping to facilitate others' spirituality, their own spiritual practice would grow and mature.

Often, the monks would come back late at night and would still be required to wake up by 4am. I was surprised at how incredibly busy their lives were, having always assumed that monastic life was supposed to be a bit more peaceful. From the time they woke up, till the time they hit the sack, it was pretty much non-stop. A ninety-minute time period was set aside during the middle of the day for studying and napping. Most monks would be able to get an hour of rest in the middle of the day and about the same amount of time was allotted for studying. I always looked forward to the precious naptime.

Gradually, I became accustomed to the daily early morning routine and the afternoon services. Even the communal setting that I had been previously apprehensive about was becoming more comfortable. My initial idea was to only be in India for a month, however, weeks and months were passing by and I was beginning to settle in.

ELABORATIONS ON THE MEDITATION PRACTICE

The meditation session was a little different than what most would expect. The first thing that comes to most people's minds when they think or hear of the word meditation is that it's probably silent. However, there are many different schools of meditation within the Hindu tradition. One method is silence, where the practitioner is trying to either still the mind, focus on the spirit soul, or focus on God within the heart. The other school of meditation deals with the utterance and repetition of mantras or sacred sound vibrations. The word "mantra" means to deliver the mind from anxieties, stresses, and fears. Hence, mantras are used to calm the mind. There are many mantras within the Hindu tradition and most are dedicated to a particular deity. The mantra can be utilized to invoke the presence and blessings of a particular deity. My grandmother and mother taught me several mantras in my childhood, and I have been reciting them ever since. The idea was that those deities would protect me in my daily endeavors. I have to admit that I did feel a connectedness to the deities and I do feel that they offered their protection.

There is a relationship that exists between the mind and the various sounds that surrounds us. When we're in deep sleep, we use the power of sound in the form of an alarm clock or a wake-up call to bring us back to reality. Different sounds and especially music have a fairly strong influence on our mind and emotions. Different types of music can put us in different moods. Utilizing this connection between sounds and our minds, mantra meditation harnesses the power of sound vibrations to benefit the mind.

The mantras are to be recited loud enough so that the individual can hear them, but not so loud that they disturb your fellow meditator. At the monastery, this would go on for about two hours. The monks would sit in circles of eight so they could help each other focus and prevent each other from dozing off. Since there were about forty monks and some working folks who would come into the temple to chant with the monks before heading off to work, there was a pretty solid murmuring sound emanating from the temple room. It was a great way to start off the day and definitely very different from eating a bowl of sugary cereal and watching cartoons or the morning news, which is what I was used to.

I'd grown up drinking a cup of tea with milk and sugar every morning, which I switched to coffee when I started working. Within a year after I started meditating seriously, I was happily able to let go of my caffeine habituation. I'm convinced that what the mind really needs is some exercise in the form of meditation and not a dose of caffeine every morning. The recommended time of day for the meditation is during the early morning hours, ideally before sunrise, which is not the only time to meditate, but is preferred. The reason for this is the mind is most relaxed and peaceful at that time and it's easier to focus on the mantra. Later in the day, the mind is easily distracted by the stimuli around it, but in the early hours there is stillness in the environment. Most of the world is sleeping and even the birds are resting, so the mind has very few things to react to.

THE MIND

One of the first things one notices upon beginning any type of meditation is just how unpredictable and wild the mind is. Sometimes it can be like the raging wind, almost as if there was a hurricane inside of our head. It's happening all the time, but it becomes very apparent when we pause to observe the mind. Even though the utterance of the mantra was quite helpful, my mind would still wander away to something else.

I'm sure many of us have questioned why the mind works the way it does, and how it comes up with all of its scattered, random and half-organized thoughts. Where are all of these thoughts coming from, and what's the reason they are there? Many of our thoughts originate from experiences we've had in the past, but the mind will also come up with dreamlike scenarios about events that have yet to take place in our lives.

We will find ourselves in a scenario for a future event, and we will be fully imagining the experience of what it would be like to live in that scenario. Some of these situations can be pleasant, while others are very nightmarish. We've all had experiences where we can be eating, sleeping, walking down the street, studying, working, listening to music or even engaging in a conversation with someone else, and the mind will begin to drift away to somewhere else. We didn't consciously decide to let the mind wander, but it did. It just left us standing there talking to someone while it decided to go away for a while.

No one willingly chooses to have a nightmare where one is chased by an animal, attacked by a murderer or falls off of a cliff. We can wake up in a sweat with our heart beating a million miles an hour. It becomes obvious that we weren't in control of our thoughts at that time, and that we are rarely ever in control of our thoughts at any time. The *Bhagavad Gita* describes the tendency of the mind as follows:

> *For him who has conquered the mind, the mind is the best of friends; but for one who has failed to do so, his mind will remain the greatest enemy.*

By referring to the mind as a friend or an enemy, the Gita treats the mind as if it were something different from us. Many times it can feel as if someone else, or even a whole group of people, is carrying on elaborate dialogues up there that have little to do with our present reality. Many Hindu texts create a distinction between the physical body, the mind, and intelligence. The mind is often compared to an impulsive child who isn't capable of making proper decisions, and the intelligence is likened to a parent that helps the mind choose the appropriate and healthy course of action.

A mind that isn't given proper attention and is allowed to run wild can cause havoc in our lives. The uncontrolled mind is the sole source of fear, stress and anger. We've all had the experience of recalling instances where others might have physically, financially or emotionally hurt us. Even though we tell ourselves that "it's over and that there's no need to continue to remember such instances," we find that the mind forcibly brings these thoughts back to the forefront of our consciousness. The Gita explains that with the help of the mind, we can either be liberated or become completely degraded. The choice is ours. It may be possible to avoid unpleasant situations, uncomfortable places or unfriendly people, but the mind isn't something we can escape. The mind lives within us and controls our thoughts, emotions and actions. We go to sleep with it every night and we wake up with it every morning. If we're going to spend that much time with someone, doesn't it make sense to develop a friendship with that individual? The question arises: How do you develop a friendship with someone that you can't see or touch or really even talk to?

First of all, we have to acknowledge that we have a mind and that we are not the mind. Second, we need to be able to admit that we have very little control over the mind's activities. Thirdly, we need to know that we're never going to have complete control over the mind. Of course, we're not talking about controlling the mind in some forceful, unnatural way. What we want to accomplish is a harmonious relationship between the mind, intelligence and the soul, so that these different components of our being can be on the same page more often. This will lead to a happier and more peaceful existence. This, of course, requires training and practice. Nothing worth achieving ever comes easy.

THE MANTRA

The mantra that the monks and the temple congregation used was from the ancient Hindu scriptures known as the Upanishads. Some teachers when giving mantras to their students prefer the students to keep them private and chant them silently. That wasn't the case with this mantra. It was very open and accessible. It consisted of only three words, but they were repeated in different combinations. It was the same mantra that I chanted while visiting the New York temple and the same one I had encountered six years ago while in Bulgaria. The mantra used was:

Hare Krishna Hare Krishna
Krishna Krishna Hare Hare
Hare Rama Hare Rama
Rama Rama Hare Hare

A lot of mantras are to one god or goddess, but this mantra was calling out to a couple, Radha and Krishna, also known as the divine couple. The word "Hare" calls out to the feminine potency and motherly nature of God known as Radha. Krishna, which means "all-attractive," refers to the masculine energy of God. Rama is a description of God known as "the reservoir of all pleasure." So, one who chants this mantra is connecting with God's feminine and masculine aspects. I definitely found this concept to be kind of cool, even though, to this day, I'm not sure I fully comprehend the concept of God being both masculine and feminine.

The goal is to audibly recite the mantra loud enough to be able to hear it. This allows the names of God to enter the mind and penetrate into the soul. This union of the mantra with the soul is called yoga. As the connection grows stronger, the envy, greed, pride, lust, and illusion that I'm this physical body starts to fade away, revealing our true spiritual identity as spiritual beings. Even though I had chanted many mantras all my life, my connection to this one seemed much more powerful and it made me feel much more connected to the divine.

Just as we're supposed to nourish our physical bodies with food and water and just as we're supposed to engage in a certain amount of exercise to keep the body healthy, similarly, we need to nourish and exercise the mind for it to remain healthy. The mantra acts as food and medicine for the mind. The mind is very much like a person. Every person is looking for a fulfilling relationship and the same is true for the mind. However, none of the relationships of this world can fully satisfy the mind so it starts looking towards things and achievements to find that satisfaction and happiness. We begin to accumulate and collect things and fill our lives with them. The problem is that the mind gets bored and tired of things very quickly and then it looks for the next new model or the next more exciting relationship. It's very important to understand that the mind's desires are unlimited and can't be satisfied by any amount of material possessions. The more it gets, the more it wants, and there's just no end. In this way, the mind keeps us always hankering and thus we always remain a bit dissatisfied.

There's a great description in the movie *The Matrix*, where Morpheus, while talking to Neo explains: "You were born into bondage...born into a prison that you cannot smell, taste, or touch—a prison for your mind." So why is a prison needed for the mind? The answer can be found by analyzing the nature of our thoughts. Most of us have had thoughts that we would be ashamed to share with others. Perhaps we've even wondered how is it that we're even capable of having such violent and criminal thoughts. Fortunately, our actions are limited due to the capacity of the body; otherwise, we would end up getting others and ourselves into a lot of trouble.

The body and the material world are like prisons for the soul and mind because we want so much more than what the material body can offer. According to the Hindu scriptures, the only thing that will satisfy the soul and mind is the reestablishment of the lost relationship with the Divine or Krishna, the all-attractive supreme. The soul is looking for a source of insatiable love and nothing in the material can provide that. That type of endless love is only available in God. That love never loses its appeal and it never becomes familiar like the love and relationships of this world.

There's no limit to the love the soul is capable of experiencing and there's no limit to the amount of love Krishna is capable of supplying. This and only this will provide the nourishment the mind and soul are looking for and this is what the mantra helps one to achieve.

The act of having to keep the mind focused as it wanders is a wonderful type of exercise for the mind. The mind is free flowing all day long. Just like anything worth accomplishing in life, it takes discipline to try to focus the mind on the mantra. The mind is so clever that it runs off to another thought and can be gone for a while before we realize that it's gone. The *Bhagavad Gita* explains:

> *From wherever the mind wanders due to its flickering and unsteady nature, one must certainly withdraw it and bring it back under the control of the self.*

Trying to focus the mind takes serious concentration and effort and after a two-hour session, even though one hasn't broken out into a sweat, it sure feels like a pretty solid workout. Sitting for two hours can be difficult on the knees, so some will stand for portions of it and some will even walk back and forth while reciting the mantra. The main focus is to hear the sound of the mantra; thus less emphasis is placed on whether one is sitting, standing, or walking. If one can sit for that long, that's probably ideal as there is a smaller chance of getting distracted. Personally, I chant for about an hour while sitting and another hour while walking. The mantra meditation is most effective if the practice is consistent. This is true of anything one is hoping to advance in. Whether it is learning to play an instrument, becoming skilled at a sport, or studying, the more consistent one becomes, the more absorption of the subject will be achieved.

Exercising the mind is a very new concept for the West. Because we're not able to see the mind when we look in the mirror, we end up completely neglecting it. We don't even realize that it has needs and that if those needs aren't met, it can become extremely unhealthy in the form of stress, anxiety, depression, sleeplessness, etc. There's nothing in this material world that can remain healthy if it's neglected. There are unlimited examples of this. Any machine will become defective if regular maintenance isn't performed. Our bodies will become dirty and unhealthy if not properly cleaned and nourished. All animate and inanimate objects of this world function in exactly the same way.

CHAPTER SIX
GUIDES AND GURUS

My desire was increasing to find a spiritual teacher who could guide me so that I could progress with more direction and guided purpose. Even though I had already adopted a daily two-hour regimen of mantra meditation, I still wanted someone who would be able to guide me through my doubts and challenges, and simultaneously inspire me to push forward in spite of obstacles. I had been listening to the lectures of different spiritual teachers to find who I felt most connected with, but it wasn't easy to choose because many were inspiring in their own unique ways.

The Hindu texts stress the importance of a spiritual guide for any serious practitioner. Many people feel that spiritual life can be practiced without a teacher. They often doubt the authenticity of a guru and are worried they might be exploited. There have always been those that pretend to be teachers in order to increase their own popularity and fame. I have met people who were disappointed by their teachers, leaving them devastated.

Unfortunately, very few people are able to open a text, spiritual or otherwise, and understand the deeper, underlying message. Whether in academia, athletics, music, or art, we have acquired the sum of our knowledge from others. A good teacher has already done successfully what we are now trying to do. They have already made the mistakes we might make and can recognize how, according to our propensities and inclinations, we can advance in the most expedient and balanced way. They do not try to control the course of our path, but involve themselves to the degree in which we as students are ready. The sixth chapter of the *Bhagavad Gita* gives good guidelines on the characteristics of a quality teacher:

> *A person is considered still further advanced when he regards honest well-wishers, affectionate benefactors, the neutral, mediators, the envious, friends and enemies, the pious and the sinners all with an equal mind.*

> *As a lamp in a windless place does not waver, so the transcendentalist, whose mind is controlled, remains always steady in his meditation on the transcendent self.*

It's also explained that if a teacher hasn't completely developed these qualities, but is actively moving in that direction, then that teacher can be trusted with one's spiritual life. A key quality of any spiritual teacher is humility. True teachers aren't proud of their spiritual advancement. They see their advancement as the mercy of God. Genuine teachers also see themselves as the servant of the student. They do not expect any kind of remuneration for the service rendered. Of course, as a matter of etiquette and reciprocation, it's also the duty of a student to try and render some service, through one's material means, to the teacher. Another key component of genuine teachers or gurus is that the messages they teach should remain consistent with the teachings of spiritual books like the *Bhagavad Gita.*

I had been living in the monastery for a couple of weeks and had yet to meet the main teacher and monk of the temple, who was the inspirational force behind everything that was taking place there. When I arrived in India, he was on a six-month tour to Europe and America. I was very curious to meet him, especially since I had been living in his temple and befriended his disciples – both monks and householders.

His name was Radhanath Swami, and he had a story like no other I had ever heard. He was an American born Jew who grew up in the suburbs of Chicago. At 19 years of age, in 1970, he left college after just one semester to go to Europe with several friends. Back then, he was known as Richard Slavin, his birth name. While traveling around Europe, he and a friend found themselves in Greece. This is where, while sitting in a cave, he heard the voice of God beckoning him to go to India. With no money in his pockets, he parted from his friends and began hitchhiking to India. He faced a variety of health problems and on several occasions found himself in dangerous cities and in life-threatening situations, but all of his trials only increased his determination to continue.

The journey to India took six months. On the way, he studied Christianity and Islam in their countries of origin. While in India, he studied the different schools of Buddhism and even met the Dalai Lama. He was deeply moved by his encounter with Mother Teresa in Calcutta, who demonstrated an attitude of deep humility and selfless service in a pursuit to bring Christ's love to the destitute and diseased of Calcutta.

He then dove into an exploration of the various aspects of Hinduism. He was particularly drawn towards the ascetic practices and chose to spend a large sum of his time living in the jungles of the Himalayan Mountains. While living in the jungles of India, he was mostly alone. Some mystics had taught him how to live and survive amongst the wild animals, explaining to him that if he didn't express or feel fear around these animals, they would not harm him.

As he traveled from one holy place to another, he met a variety of teachers who offered him guidance and from whom he learned various techniques of yoga and meditation. Prior to coming to India, he had never met an Indian person or been exposed to the Hindu religion. The culture and the religion were all very new, but somehow, he was naturally attracted to the yogic lifestyle. The adventures he underwent, the teachers and guides he met and studied with, and the practices he engaged in are elaborately described in his autobiography *The Journey Home*. He now runs a temple called the Radha-Gopinath Temple, located near Chowpatty beach in Mumbai. It houses almost 200 monks and serves a congregation of over 5,000 members. He has inspired a food relief program, which serves 200,000 under-privileged kids in and around Mumbai on a daily basis. His guidance has also helped to develop the Bhaktivedanta Hospital in Mumbai, which provides treatment incorporating both Eastern and Western medicines and techniques.

I had a chance to meet him very briefly when he arrived back in Mumbai after his European and American tour. I knocked on his door and introduced myself. He asked me if I was comfortable in the monastery and I told him I was. I thanked him for creating such a warm and wonderful environment for people to come and take shelter. He folded his hands together in the prayerful way they do in India when people say "Namaste." I offered my respects by folding my hands in the same way. I didn't have any more conversations with him during the rest of my trip, but I attended his lectures within and outside the temple. I felt great inspiration in my heart just listening to him speak. He spoke with such honesty and conviction about the nature of reality and the courage and devotion required to grow spiritually. His words resonated with me in the deepest and most heartfelt of ways.

I felt very inspired by the divine calling of Radhanath Swami and his relentless pursuit of it, as well as the touching way in which he had guided and trained so many qualified people in their spiritual practice. I could sense that he embodied so many of the genuine qualities of a real teacher. I was inspired to become his student. I was listening to the lectures of many gurus and teachers, but there was something about his presence and depth that penetrated my heart and soul in a way that is difficult to describe. However, it would take me another six months or so before I would officially approach him during one of his visits to America and ask if I could become his student and he my teacher. The relationship between a student and teacher is a serious one and I wanted to ensure that I was ready to commit. I didn't want to rush into it and later change my mind. Within Hinduism, this relationship is as important if not more than a commitment one makes at the time of marriage. So, I needed to think about it.

After spending almost three months in the temple, I decided to visit Vrindavana, the birthplace of Krishna. My trip had already gone over by two months. I had left at the end of September and now it was close to the end of December and the year was coming to a close. My original plan was to be in India for about a month. I didn't even know if I would last that long. Three months had passed. My parents were becoming a little antsy about my extended trip. They weren't overtly pushing me to return, but their subtle hints were emotionally felt. They would express that it would be nice to have me back to help out with the family business.

It was impossible for me to ignore the calling to discover life, God, and myself. The meditation, the devotion, and the deep genuine camaraderie I had experienced at the temple were like no other. I had had gracious, caring friendships in high school and college, but nothing compared to the depth of the friendships I had developed with these monks. It's not easy to express what one goes through when they receive a calling to seek out the truth about life and death. I don't know how easy or difficult it is for people who don't have that calling to understand what one is experiencing. Being surrounded by people who could understand what I was going through, because they themselves were going through it, was exhilarating and also comforting.

CHAPTER SEVEN

WHERE GOD WALKED THE EARTH

Every other year, the Radha-Gopinath temple organizes a pilgrimage for most of the monks and congregation to Vrindavana. The year I went, about 1,000 people attended. People came from West and East Europe, Africa, South America, and America. For 10 to 12 days, the group would either take buses or walk to holy places where holy persons had visited or God incarnate had actually walked and performed activities. Nowadays, the group numbers have increased to 4,000 participants per trip!

It was a powerful experience. I had never traveled with that many people before. The trip felt austere at times because 1,000 of us traveled together, but ecstatic because of the religious sites we would visit. We endured chilling cold baths in Northern India during the autumn months of October and November. The staying accommodations included a simple room with an attached bathroom. The bathrooms had no showers in them. Instead, there was a tap four feet off the floor and you had two choices: either fill the bucket and pour a mug full of cold water on yourself, or sit underneath the tap. I would usually choose the bucket option because the tap flow wasn't that strong and was like slow torture. At least with the mug, I could quickly pour a few mugs, soap myself down, repeat the process, and be done with it. You also had to wash your clothes in the cold water, and I found that getting soap out of my clothes was quite a challenge. Taking cold baths in Bombay was refreshing because it's almost always 80 degrees and humid.

The toilets were Indian style, which meant that they were inserted into the ground and you had to squat over them. It required a good deal of flexibility to respond to nature's call with these toilets, and I had a hard time squatting that low. Sometimes in our travel between villages, there would be no toilet facility at all. I had to learn how to find a bush in a somewhat distant place, squat down and take care of business. In addition to making sure I was alone, I was a little paranoid and carefully watched for small animals and insects crawling around me. Many villages have hand pumps in different locations where the locals can pump out water and use it for bathing or washing clothes. I don't know how I managed, but I came to enjoy the "all-natural" experience of performing activities of daily living outdoors. It felt like an adventure.

Custom says that when you're in a holy place for the purpose of performing a pilgrimage, you walk barefoot. Toward the end of our 10-day trip, walking on pebbles and even thorns in my bare feet was starting to take its toll. I still remember the relief when the trip ended and I could once again wear my flip-flops. I realized how simple comforts, such as having footwear, could be so rewarding. At the same time, I had enjoyed the ascetic experience.

The buses we used to travel to and from one place to another were referred to as "luxury buses." When I heard the term, I expected something at least as comfortable as a Greyhound, but it turned out that the word "luxury" was grossly misleading. A lot of the windows didn't close all the way, letting in all kinds of dust and smoke from other vehicles. The shock absorbers were non-existent and the seats in front of you didn't have proper padding on the back so your shins would knock up against the bare metal. Every time the bus hit a bump, it launched you up and brought you slamming back down against hard seats. I imagined that American prison buses would be more comfortable. However, I tried to keep in mind that bodily comfort should be ignored during these pilgrimages. The same things that made the experience challenging also provided a lot of inspiration and strength.

Being with so many people who really wanted to challenge themselves in these difficult circumstances was quite inspiring. I admired their eagerness to see the places and listen to the lectures. Most of these people worked regular jobs and were using their vacation time to go on pilgrimage. Usually vacation is an opportunity for respite or comfort, but these people were instead taking an opportunity to explore their spirituality. They were from all walks of life, from the very wealthy to those from low-income families. I was amazed that no one was given privileges over anyone else, except for the elderly and the disabled.

Many would end up getting sick by the time the pilgrimage was over, but there were typically no expressions of regret on anyone's face. They knew what to expect and they were enthusiastic throughout the entire time. I definitely felt a certain inner strength after the pilgrimage was over and saw the benefit of such an intensive retreat. Prior to my pilgrimage, I had certain experiences of God through meditation; but after visiting the many places where Krishna had performed his activities and exchanged interactions with his devotees, my realization of the existence and personality of God had intensified, and my faith increased.

SICK IN VRINDAVANA

Vrindavana is a town where one can make a lot of spiritual advancement. It is recommended that the trip is only three days long to maximize the individual focus, and so as to prevent the visitor from becoming familiar with the place and the people. It is argued that through familiarity the visitor will become critical of the surroundings.

I was also told to avoid developing a frivolous mentality. The purpose of the trip was to go deeper into my prayer and meditation, render services to the people and in temples, study scriptures, and bathe in the holy river Yamuna. The mood shouldn't be one of wanting to go shopping in the very popular Loi bazaar where one can make purchases for a pretty good bargain. One also shouldn't be visiting Vrindavana to enjoy eating the variety of foods it has to offer. It's this last, yet significant, piece of advice that I ignored and ended up paying a heavy price during a trip to Vrindavana a few years later.

During the second visit, I met a few student monks whom I had known from back when I had visited the New York temple. They invited me to dinner at this very cool restaurant that served pizza and a lot of American dishes. After having eating Indian food for a couple of months, I was ready for some good American food. When I first walked in, I felt like I was back in the U.S. There was exposed brick and nice wooden tables. The place was packed with mostly Westerners and some Indians. Six or eight of us got a table and ordered pizzas with extra toppings, French fries, veggie burgers, sodas, and ice cream. When the food arrived, we dove in. We ate, laughed, joked, and had a fantastic time. I assumed that since this food was American, my system should easily be able to deal with it and digest it. I was wrong! It looked and tasted like American food, but the quality wasn't the same. Sometime around midnight, I woke up with diarrhea. At some point, I became so dehydrated that I started feeling light-headed and felt as if I were sweating. That stopped within a few moments, but then I started feeling nauseous. While still on the toilet, I quickly grabbed the bucket and started to regurgitate everything I had eaten. I returned to my bed after 20 minutes of this, but spent the night running to the bathroom every several hours. When morning arrived, I had been thoroughly depleted of all liquids and energy. I laid in bed feeling even worse than when I had gotten sick during my first trip to India. I remained in bed drinking water the rest of the day. By the end of the day, I was able to eat some rice with yogurt, which serves to bind the stomach. Amazingly, I recovered quickly and by the next day I was fine.

While I was in bed, I contemplated the warning I had gotten from many about not going to Vrindavana with the intention to enjoy the material facilities it had to offer. It's not a place to go with a vacationing spirit. This was a valuable lesson and one that I still remember very vividly. Every time I go to Vrindavana, I try to only stay for about three days and have a game plan chalked out as to which temples I want to visit, which lectures I want to hear, and what books I will read. Once the mind has a set and purposeful intention, it has a better chance at avoiding distraction.

RADHARANI

Vrindavana is unique amongst the holy places in India because it not only recognizes God as a combination of masculine and feminine energy, but it also places the emphasis on the feminine side of the divine. The feminine aspect of the divine is called Radharani.

Radharani descended from the spiritual realm shortly after Krishna, approximately 5,000 years ago. She was born in the small village Barsana, which is about twenty-eight miles from Mathura, the birthplace of Krishna. The word Radha comes from the Sanskrit verbal roots "radh," which means to worship, and "rani," which means queen, so Radharani can be literally translated to mean "the queen of worship." In some texts, she is described as "the supreme goddess who can be worshipped by everyone. She is the protector of all, and she is the mother of the entire universe."

The answer to the question that has been on everyone's mind for millennia is, YES & NO. The question is: *Is God a Man*? God is not just male, and according to some Vedic scriptures, God has both masculine and feminine expansions. In the 10th chapter of the *Bhagavad Gita*, Krishna alludes to his feminine traits, *"Among women I am fame, fortune, fine speech, memory, intelligence, steadfastness and patience."*

However, in some of the more esoteric texts such as the *Puranas* and the *Chaitanya-Caritamrita*, it explains that the complete manifestation of God includes his feminine counterpart, Radha. Inconceivably, they are both one and separate, as Krishna expanded himself into two for the purpose of exchanging love. There is a beautiful description in the *Chaitanya-Caritamrita*, which gives us a window into the connection between Radha and Krishna:

> *Sri Radha is the full power, and Lord Krishna is the possessor of full power. The two are not different, as evidenced by the revealed scriptures. They are indeed the same, just as musk and its scent are inseparable, or as fire and its heat are non-different. Thus Radha and Krishna are one, yet they have taken two forms to enjoy the mellows of pastimes.*

This concept is not an easy one to grasp. If God is full and complete, why does he need to expand himself to exchange love? God has a personality, which indicates that he has preferences. Perhaps this need to expand for the purpose of exchanging love speaks of the importance love plays in the lives of all individuals. Our desire to love and be loved comes from God. For the most part, no one wants to be alone, at least not permanently. The thing everyone is chasing after is love. We all want to know that there are people out there that love us. Simultaneously, we hanker to be able to give our love to others.

Here are additional passages from the *Caitanya-Caritamrita* describing Radha's qualities and love for Krishna. "Radharani's body, mind, and words are steeped in love for Krishna…The body of Radharani is a veritable transformation of love of Godhead. Even

Krishna can't understand the strength of Radha's love, which overwhelms Him. Her transcendental body is complete with unparalleled spiritual qualities. Even Lord Krishna Himself cannot reach the limit of the transcendental qualities of Radharani." These are some of Radha's prominent qualities:

- *Radha is adolescent and always freshly youthful*
- *Radha is very sweet and most charming to look at*
- *Radha's face is smiling and ever blissful*
- *Radharani is the most exceptional singer and vina player*
- *Radha's words are charming and pleasing*
- *Radha is exceptionally humble*
- *Radha is the embodiment of mercy and compassion*
- *Radha possesses Mahabhava, the highest sentiments of love*
- *Radha always keeps Krishna under Her control; Krishna submissively obeys Radha's command*

These topics of divine and spiritual love between Radha and Krishna will always remain a mystery as long as we remain on the material platform. Love on the spiritual level is devoid of selfishness. The needs and interests of the other take precedence over one's own needs. The earthly love closest to spiritual love is that of a mother towards her child. It is full of sacrifice and is completely selfless; it is without expectation. The feeling of love is derived from the service itself. The child is limited in its capacity to reciprocate with the mother's love. Even if it increases its demands, the mother will continue giving. For most, we can only imagine a relationship where the reciprocation of love and service is completely selfless and without expectation. It's the kind of love our hearts hanker for. By eradicating selfishness and incorporating selflessness, the path of *bhakti,* or devotional service, prepares one's heart and consciousness to understand and experience that divine love which exists between Radha and Krishna.

After the Vrindavana pilgrimage ended, the pilgrims returned to their respective cities. There were some monks from New York that were planning on spending time in Vrindavana, and I decided to share a room with the two of them. One of them was Robert, with whom I would end up living in the Manhattan monastery a few months later. Since we weren't living in the temple complex, we had the flexibility of creating an independent schedule, which was quite different than in the Mumbai temple, where everyone got up together and went through half the day together. I would need to chalk out my own schedule and figure out how I would engage myself. The morning services in Vrindavana started at 4:15 a.m. as opposed to 5:00 a.m. in Mumbai, which meant I would need to wake up by 3:45 a.m. This was definitely more challenging, but I was determined to follow through. Everyday, I would wake up at 3:45 a.m., turn on the water heater, take a warm shower, and walk out into the unlit alleyway leading to the temple.

Once during my morning walk to the temple, I saw a giant ox walking down the dark alley towards my housing complex. Oxen are fairly mild in behavior and mind their own business, but they also have huge horns and like to swing their head side to side as they walk. I considered just walking by it as most people do, but decided not to take any chances. It was dark and I didn't want to startle it in any way, but at the same time, I didn't want to be late for the morning prayers. I chose safety over punctuality and decided to wait until the big guy passed.

VRINDAVANA AND THE MORNING PROGRAM

Up to 100 people attended the first part of the morning service. During the festival season in October and November, attendance increases to several hundred people. Many temples in Vrindavana start their morning service by 4:00 or 4:30 a.m. or even earlier, so one can hear bells, gongs, and singing happening right from the early morning hours. Vrindavana is the land of 5,000 temples, mostly dedicated to Krishna, and is located in an area of about 150 square miles. It's approximately 90 miles south of Delhi. During that trip, I learned that in India whether you're in a train, a taxi, bus, house, or a public place such as a temple, there is no such thing as "maximum occupancy limit." People cram into spaces to the point where everyone is pushed left and right, and then they cram some more. If you're not used to this, it can be claustrophobic. The crowds tested my patience and tolerance.

During this festival season, many hundreds were showing up for the morning service. I remember folding my hands while looking up at the altar at 4:30 a.m. in the morning, trying to muster up whatever devotion I could from the bottom of my heart, and getting shoved. There is nothing like a good shove at 4:30 in the morning to knock the devotion right out of your system. I was tempted to shove back. Growing up in the road rage culture of Los Angeles, if someone cuts you off, you return the favor. However, I had to remind myself that I couldn't let my intolerance overcome me in this environment. Most of the attendees were local village people and were accustomed to pushing and shoving. So, I allowed myself to get moved around by the crowd. I found it amazing that they weren't disturbed by all the commotion; on the contrary, the chaos seemed to increase their devotion. It seemed as if this difficulty was the price to pay to be in the temple, and that it was worth it. I realized I had a long ways to go to come to their level of tolerance and patience. The American phenomena this can be likened to is a rock concert or "Black Friday," the biggest shopping day of the year when people wait outside stores before they open and are ready to trample over each just to make a purchase. The difference is that during the month-long Kartik celebration, this is a daily affair and the goal is to increase one's devotion.

KARTIK

The month of Kartik takes place during the middle to the end of October and spills into November. The dates are calculated according to the lunar calendar, and therefore change each year, but it's usually during October and November. The reason there is such a frenzy in Vrindavana is because the scriptures and teachers of the past explain that any spiritual activities performed during this month in Vrindavana are multiplied 1,000 times by Krishna. People who are eager to make spiritual advancement and those looking to gain something materially come to Vrindavana to engage in meditation, donate money, or provide physical service to the locals and the temples. The idea is that God will bestow mercy upon those who are sincerely endeavoring for spiritual growth. This theme is communicated through the recitation of a popular story about Lord Krishna.

Krishna, during his infancy, feeling hungry, broke a pot of butter and started eating the freshly churned butter that his mother had worked very hard to produce. She decided that in order for her to finish her household duties and keep Krishna from any further mischief, she would take a thin rope and tie one end around Krishna's waist and the other end to a grinding mortar.

My mom told me that when I was just a toddler, she would tie a small rope to one of my ankles and the other to a fixed object so she could keep an eye on me while she worked in the kitchen. She had done this after I had gotten into the kitchen and placed my palm onto a burning hot stove, so I related to this part of the story.

Yasoda, Krishna's mother, gathered together some rope, but when she tried to wrap it around Krishna's belly, the rope was two inches too short. She got more rope and eventually got all the rope from the farm, tied the ends together, but it still wouldn't make it around Krishna's belly and was again two inches short. Ultimately, Krishna allowed her to bind him up and the reason for this was that she had pure love for him and he succumbed to her desire to bind him. The deeper meaning here is that he allowed himself to be bound up by her love.

The first inch represents a devotee's endeavor to love God and the other inch represents God's mercy towards the devotee. In order to develop pure, unmotivated love for God, one has to use one's free will to endeavor to love God and if one does, God will surely reciprocate.

There are devotees who truly will themselves with all their capacity to express their love for God. Some who were really hardcore would wake up at 2:00 a.m. or 3:00 a.m. to start meditating. The program began with one person leading the morning prayers, which consisted of a song glorifying the spiritual teachers accompanied by two Indian instruments, cymbals and a Bengali drum called the *mridanga*. As the rhythm and momentum increased, the participants would start to sway side to side. When the tempo reached its height, people would begin dancing around in a circle with their arms raised. Some would even begin jumping up and down in ecstasy. This would go on for about thirty minutes. There were two more short songs, adding up to an hour of singing and dancing.

The next part of the program involved mantra meditation. In all the temples I visited and in the one I live in New York, this was and continues to be the more challenging part of the morning service because there's no singing and no musical instruments. Only three parties are involved during this session – you, your mind, and the mantra. Many people doze off during this portion of the program. Unless you've had a good night's sleep, the one and a half to two hour session can get kind of rough. It's even more intense if you had a long and tiring day prior. The mind absolutely refuses to cooperate. Even though we consciously know that the mind and body are separate entities, there is a strong relationship between the two: the body affects the mind and the mind affects the body. Some people have body types that just can't stay awake while sitting and chanting, so you can see their heads bobbing which means they're going in and out of sleep. Some people, to prevent from falling asleep, will stand and chant, but I've even seen people start to fall asleep while standing. It's these times I wonder what's more distracting, my mind or the bobbing heads.

Fortunately, I've never really had a problem staying awake during the meditation. This doesn't mean I'm any better than anyone else—everyone has his or her own challenges. Because I have an active body and mind, my challenge is that my mind races from one thing to another and can't focus on the sound of the mantra, which is the goal of the meditation. During the meditation, I can't sit for more than thirty to forty-five minutes and after awhile have to walk back and forth.

After the meditation session is over, more prayers are sung and then a member of the community delivers a 45 minute to an hour-long lecture from the *Srimad Bhagavatam* (*Bhagavat Purana*). A different person speaks each day. The lecturer recites a verse and commentary from the scripture, and then shares his or her own thoughts and realizations from that verse. This is another portion of the program where you can see people taking naps but it's usually not voluntarily. A lot of the time people who know they're going to doze will be considerate enough to sit towards the back of the temple, but some, out of their genuine enthusiasm to listen to the class will sit right up front and start to fall asleep right in front of the speaker.

When I started lecturing, I realized how easy it was to spot people who were falling asleep. No matter where in the audience they may be, I always noticed if someone was sitting with their eyes closed and head tilted to one side. It's even more distracting if a person sitting right in front of you starts nodding off. I usually try to ignore sleepers and engage with the more alert members of the audience, but sometimes I'll try to look at the person with the hope that they will keep their eyes open. Sometimes this works, but usually it's not effective.

I remember in the 1980s, there was a commercial for the U.S. army that used to play in between programs on television. It depicted soldiers at the crack of dawn parachuting out of airplanes, busily getting into jeeps, driving off for an exciting mission, and then sitting with the team and having a cup of coffee. The slogan sung during the commercial was "we do more before 9:00 a.m. than most people do all day." After a few months of attending the morning program, for some reason this slogan popped into my head and I started to feel as if my life resembled it. By nine o'clock, I had chanted, danced, battled the mind, heard a lecture on spiritual topics, and had eaten a hearty, healthy breakfast.

Prior to joining the monastery, I would roll out of bed at around 7:00 a.m., brush my teeth, grab a box of cereal and cold milk from the fridge and sit in front of the television. During my teens, especially on weekends and during summer break from school, I wouldn't get out of bed until 11:00 a.m. or even later and then just hang out with my friends. I wouldn't go to sleep until about 1:00 a.m. or later. My appreciation for the early morning hours of the day and how they positively influenced the mind greatly increased.

After attending most of the morning program, I would get some hot ginger milk served in a clay mug from a stand across the street and grab some fruits, nuts, and some bread cake. I'd take my breakfast up to the roof of the place where I was staying and would enjoy it underneath the bright, warm sun. Afterward, I would go down to my room and take a short nap, then go back up to the roof and open up the *Bhagavad Gita*, which I would study until 12:30 p.m. Lunch was at 1:00 p.m. and I didn't want to be late for that. During the afternoon, I would visit the tombs of some prominent teachers of the "Bhakti" tradition. Many had resided here and had decided to spend the last stage of their lives here. Since Vrindavana is a place where Krishna personally appeared and is considered as one of the holiest places in India, many people retire here in their old age.

THE PURPOSE OF YOGA

This was the first time after my initial exposure to the *Gita* in Bulgaria that I engaged in an in-depth study of the *Gita*. I obtained a study guide and recorded lectures from teachers who had extensively explained the entirety of the *Gita*. During my one-month stay in Vrindavana, I went to the roof everyday to study the *Gita* for three hours, alternating between reading the text, the study guide, and listening to the lectures on my walkman. I learned that the *Gita* is divided up into three sections of six chapters each – Karma (work) yoga, Bhakti (devotion) yoga, and Jnana (knowledge) yoga. I was surprised to learn that none of these three types of yoga had anything to do with the physical postures. The word yoga is derived from the Sanskrit "yuj," which means to yoke, unite, or join. In a spiritual context, the word yoga means to unite the soul with God; thus, the three types of yoga mentioned in the Gita are three ways through which one can reach a union with Krishna, the speaker of the Gita. Chapter six of the Gita explains:

> *A person is said to be elevated in yoga when, having renounced all material desires, he neither acts for sense gratification nor engages in fruitive activities.*

For one whose mind is unbridled, self-realization is difficult work. But he whose mind is controlled and who strives by appropriate means is assured of success. That is My opinion.

The ancient histories are full of narratives in which individuals of all walks of life engage in physical yoga practice combined with breathing techniques to eventually pacify the mind so that it could meditate on God. Before one could realize the truth of God's presence, yoga was supposed to facilitate removing the false ego in order for one to realize that he or she is not the physical body or mind, rather an eternal spiritual being. The traditional yoga path was quite arduous. Below there is a sample of the conventional yoga practice as described in the sixth chapter of the *Gita*. It's important to note that Arjuna rejected this practice because he saw it as "impractical" and "unendurable."

To practice yoga, one should go to a secluded place and should lay kusa grass on the ground and then cover it with a deerskin and a soft cloth. The seat should be neither too high nor too low and should be situated in a sacred place. The yogi should then sit on it very firmly and practice yoga to purify the heart by controlling his mind, senses and activities and fixing the mind on one point. One should hold one's body, neck and head erect in a straight line and stare steadily at the tip of the nose. Thus, with an undisturbed, subdued mind, devoid of fear, completely free from sex life, one should meditate upon Me within the heart and make Me the ultimate goal of life.

Arjuna, being a man of the world with family and responsibility, realized that this form of yoga practice, stripped of material comforts, is for those rare individuals who are ready to renounce the world and everything it has to offer. Arjuna wasn't prepared for that degree of renunciation, so Krishna offered him other options such as Karma, Bhakti, and Jnana through which Arjuna could attain union with the Divine. When I first read this description, while in Bulgaria, I thought the *Gita* was prescribing renunciation and sitting in stillness. I felt at the time that I would not be able to realistically exercise these practices regularly. There was no way I would be able to sit for more than 10 minutes with my head, body, and neck erect—I grew up sitting on couches and lazy boy recliners. I found myself agreeing with Arjuna, and wanted a way to remain involved in the world while simultaneously making spiritual advancement at a comfortable pace.

The word "bhakti" means devotion to God. Some teachers have expanded the meaning of "bhakti" to mean devotional service to God, believing that devotion to God is complete when complemented by service to God. Developing bhakti or love of God is the highest pursuit recommended by the *Gita*. One Hindu scripture called the *Srimad Bhagavatam* suggests that nothing other than bhakti should be the goal of our lives. It's further explained that we've been wandering through the various species of life, being born, growing old, and dying, millions and millions of times, and have finally attained a human form which affords us the capacity to inquire about the important questions of life: Who are we? What is God? What is our ultimate purpose? The human life is considered to be a gift because it allows us to not only ask the questions, but also engage in spiritual practices that can liberate the soul from the physical body and the material world.

Bhakti exists in all traditions of the world, and is not exclusive to Hinduism. Any tradition that teaches its practitioners to engage in loving service to the divine is teaching bhakti. The ideal practice of bhakti involves serving without an ulterior motive. We shouldn't be asking for something material in exchange for our devotion; otherwise, worship becomes a business deal. The *Srimad Bhagavatam*, a Hindu text, recommends that we gradually come to a platform where our bhakti is completely unmotivated.

While I sat at the tombs of the great teachers, I found meditation and prayer to be especially introspective. It is explained that if one prays with sincerity for spiritual advancement at these tombs, one can feel the presence and receive the blessings of that saint. Some of the most powerful experiences of meditation that I have ever had were in front of the tombs of these great and pure-hearted personalities.

According to the *Gita* and Hindu philosophy, death isn't the end of everything. It is a gateway to new beginnings. The West has a very different outlook on death than the East. The East sees life as a cycle as opposed to the linear model typical of the West. According to one's activities (*karma*), one's soul will continue its journey through different material bodies until the achievement of liberation from the material world. The great saints are considered liberated even while residing in the body, so their death isn't viewed in the same way as a non-liberated person's death. Of course, one doesn't have to be at the tombs to pray to the great teachers and saints to receive their blessings. One can reach out to them from anywhere at anytime and feel connected. After visiting the tombs during the afternoon, I would attend philosophical discourses or join in a *kirtan* (devotional singing) session in the evenings.

Vrindavana is known for its wild monkeys. The monkeys can be seen on the raised walls or swinging from tree to tree—they act as if they own the town. They are somewhat cautious around locals but are pretty fearless around foreigners. The locals won't hesitate to whack them with a stick. If you walk down the street with groceries, you can be sure to attract the attention of a monkey clan—they'll rip the bag of food right out of your hands baring their teeth. They move with such stealth that often the victim won't even realize that they've been robbed of their food.

They're also known as great bargainers, as I came to experience firsthand in the Loi Bazaar, the town market. The local shopkeepers there who sell fruits and vegetables in the open carry and wave sticks around to keep the monkeys away. The locals explain that if you're carrying a stick while you walk around, the monkeys won't bother you. I didn't know this, and one day I was standing in the middle of a narrow street lined with small houses, when a monkey jumped down in front of me, took my eyeglasses right off my face, and jumped up onto a balcony on the other side of the street. I could feel his fingers graze my face, but he didn't scratch me.

It happened so quickly that I was caught off guard, and it's usually not a good idea to resist because they can get vicious very quickly. He sat on the balcony holding my glasses while looking down at me. I'm pretty blind without my glasses, so I was panicking and worrying that I would need to get a new pair. Fortunately, I was with a monk who had spent a lot of time in India, especially Vrindavana, and had become acquainted with the bargaining techniques of the monkeys. He quickly got a banana and threw it up to the monkey. The monkey happily grabbed the banana, dropped my glasses on the balcony, and took off. We knocked on the door of the house and the homeowner returned my glasses to me.

MAYAPUR

I had heard of some courses and seminars on the scriptures being offered in a temple near Calcutta. Up until now I had been only studying the *Gita* independently and through lectures, so I decided that I wanted to study the texts in a more systematic way.

It was late in December 1999 and it was getting foggy and cold in Vrindavana. If you aren't used to it, the winters can be brutal. There's no indoor heating anywhere. There are space heaters, but they're only in some rooms and all the homes are made of stone, so everything is cold. The temple room is cold, the cafeterias and restaurants are cold, even the hotel rooms are cold.

I decided to head off to Mayapur, which was about 100 kilometers from Calcutta. Mayapur was located in an area known as Navadvip, or the "the nine islands." The weather was a bit more tropical, so even though it was cold in the mornings and evenings, it would warm up really nicely during the day. I would bathe in the Ganges river, which flowed about 100 yards from the temple compound.

Even though the Mayapur monkeys were about twice the size of the monkeys in Vrindavana and could leap like Spiderman, they never bothered anyone or tried to steal your food. In Mayapur, the mosquitoes were the problem. If you didn't use some kind of mosquito repellant and wear socks, especially in the mornings and evening, they would gang up and feast on you. Luckily, these mosquitoes didn't have malaria like the ones in Bombay. If they did, I'd probably be dead. I lost count of the times I was bitten before I started taking the necessary precautions.

I went from living with forty monks in Bombay, to living with two familiar faces in Vrindavana, to living alone in Mayapur. Even though I didn't have siblings, I always had my parents around, so up until now I had not lived independently. I found the solitude challenging. I had enrolled in a few scriptural courses that were being offered in the temple at Mayapur. I would attend the entire morning program from 4:30 a.m. to 9:00 a.m., eat breakfast, take a short nap, then attend the 90 minute long discourse.

Mayapur was a little village and there wasn't a whole lot to do other than meditate, pray, and visit temples. To keep busy, I took short, half-day pilgrimages and visited nearby temples, meditated, studied scripture, and bathed in the Ganges. I nearly drowned in the river. A few friends had visited from the West on a festival day, and we decided to go swimming. Where we were swimming, the Ganges had small patches of land in the water, and we were leisurely swimming from patch to patch. It was late in the afternoon, the sun was hot, and I was weak and tired from fasting for the festival. Suddenly I grew distant from the nearest patch. Halfway to land, I felt my body succumb to exhaustion and I began to sink. I started praying to Chaitanya, the saint born here. Just after my head submerged, my feet touched sand. I was safe and alive. I couldn't help but feel the hand and protection of Chaitanya in my life during that moment.

Everyday, breakfast and lunch were served in the cafeteria of the compound, and a huge crowd of at least 100 people would attend. It was always an event! The plates and bowls we ate with were made out of banana leaves, and spoons weren't necessary because everyone ate with their hands. The unique thing about the Bengali people and their diet is their love of rice. I thought I loved rice, but I was utterly humbled at their level of consumption. A server would bring around rice first, and they wouldn't even wait for the soup or vegetable—they would dive straight into the rice. Growing up in a North Indian family, we ate our rice towards the end of the meal and we never ate it by itself. I was used to eating rice with soup or a vegetable dish. I would wait patiently until another item came before beginning my meal.

I would satisfy my appetite for non-Indian food by frequenting the pizza and cake stand, which was also visited by the large Western populace, residents, and spiritual tourists. In the evenings, I would go on top of one of the buildings and watch the sun set over the Ganges.

VISITING EKACHAKRA

During my stay in Mayapur, I decided to visit a nearby holy place located in West Bengal. The town was known as Ekachakra, and it was the birth place of a great 15th century saint named Nityananda. You could walk from one end of the town to another in about 20 minutes. The town consisted of palm trees, dirt roads, mud and straw huts. Cows and goats shared the road with the very small population. Cars, vehicles, and electricity were almost non-existent. The village people milked cows and lived a very natural life without any technology. From what I could tell, there was no indoor plumbing. If you wanted to bathe, you had to pump water out of the well into a bucket, and that would be your bath. Having grown up around so much technology and convenience, I was surprisingly thrilled to be here.

We slept in a room that was still under construction. It had no doors or windows. There were bails of hay for our beds, so I put my sleeping bag on top of some hay and went to sleep. You went to sleep when it got dark, since without electricity there was no light and not much to do. I was relishing this simple life. My mind felt so peaceful and quiet. I didn't have a million thoughts running through it. Now, I could understand how our fast-paced Western lives, full of gadgets and activities, drive us to work ourselves into a frenzy. Our surroundings can disturb our minds.

Once, in the middle of the night, I could hear a fluttering sound that I soon discovered were bats flying in and out of the room. I freaked out. It was about two in the morning, and having seen a few too many vampire flicks, I realized there was no way I could again fall asleep. I decided to get up, bathe, and start my morning meditation. With the help of my flashlight, I made my way to the well, where I pumped out a bucket full of water and started to bathe. The water was slightly cool, but I loved it. The full moon shone in the dark night and I was so excited to be bathing in the open air under the cooling light of the moon. I quickly put on my robes and made my way to the roof to start my meditation by 3:00 a.m. It was the earliest I had ever woken for meditation—or for any morning ritual at that. There were absolutely no sounds or distractions. Sitting there in the still of the early morning hours, with the moon shining above, I took hold of my beads and started to chant. The quality of my meditation was probably one of the best I've ever experienced. It was a short but very sweet trip to Ekachakra, and I was very grateful for the chance to visit this very serene and holy place. I then returned to Mayapur.

Spending so much time alone with myself and my mind brought up a lot of intense questioning. What did this whole experience in India really mean for me? Could I actually pursue some of these spiritual practices when I returned to the West? I really needed to figure out what I was going to do with the rest of my life. I had two months left on my visa, and I knew that I would have to go back to the U.S.

Even though these experiences were enriching, I questioned whether I was being responsible or using spiritual life as an escape from reality. I decided that regardless of this, my experiences were still deep and powerful. I had no desire to go back to life as usual. Working a nine to five job with people seeking material success was no longer my idea of a fulfilling life.

My mom was visiting India and staying in Kanpur with her relatives at the time. She wanted to come with her aunt to Mayapur to visit me. It had been five months since I'd been away from home, the longest she'd been away from me. She and her aunt traveled all the way from Kanpur to see me. It took them almost an entire day's travel by train and bus. During their short trip, I showed them around the town and some of the temples and tombs in the area.

I had a week left before my six-month visa expired, and I decided to spend it in the Bombay temple. Having lived in a couple of other communities, I was amazed at the strength of support every member of the community was given here. I immediately felt sheltered. I understood how much one's relationships within a community affect one's faith. To help newer monks and community members deal with personal or faith related issues, the Bombay temple has a system where more seasoned members of the community are encouraged to make themselves available and act as mentors and friends.

With a sad heart, I left Bombay and all the friends I had made in India. I wasn't sure what I was going back to in America. I wasn't eager to get another full-time job, and I wasn't excited about working with my father. I decided that instead of returning immediately to my parents' house, I would spend some time in the Manhattan monastery in New York City and then decide on my next course of action.

CHAPTER EIGHT

URBAN MONK IN TRAINING

Returning to America was an unexpected culture shock. After living such a simple life without television, internet, radio, and other technology, I had become quite comfortable with a slow-paced lifestyle. I hadn't committed to the monastic order since I wasn't certain I could live out my life this way. Completely immersing myself in spiritual culture was like bathing away my confusions and uncertainties. I knew I would have to take it one day at a time.

My father wanted me to go home and spend some time with the family, but I felt inclined to go straight to the New York monastery. This wasn't easy for my parents, as they had expected me to move back home with them. I know it was heartbreaking for my mother because, like most mothers, she wanted me to always be close to her. However, I had just undergone the most powerful six months of my life, and felt quite strongly that I shouldn't disrupt my spiritual momentum in any way. I knew there was more that I needed to discover about myself and more that I needed to learn. My journey wasn't complete.

The experience in New York was very different from the one in India. Up until now, I had lived in New Jersey, and this was the first time that I would be living in New York. Compared to Bombay and other major cities in India, New York is not nearly as

121

stressful. Primarily, everything is cleaner, down to the air. In Mumbai, none of the cars have a proper exhaust system, so they pump out dark black exhaust into the air everyone breathes. The worst part is when you're in one of those motorized three-wheeled auto-rickshaws with no doors or windows and you inhale everything from all the vehicles. I was horrified the first time I blew my nose after a day around Mumbai and saw black grit in the tissue. Some of the local monks said that walking around Mumbai for a day is like smoking a half a pack of cigarettes.

A European monk who had been raised as a Christian started the monastery in Manhattan in 1997. He was in his late 30s and had been a monk for over 15 years. The first place he had acquired was a tiny one-bedroom apartment on Fifth Street and Bowery. It was so small that I was convinced it was a studio turned into a one-bedroom to extract more rent. In the beginning, he lived there with two monks who he was training. In a little over a year some well wishers pitched in and he was able to upgrade to a three-bedroom on Fourth Street and First Avenue.

They called the new space the Bhaktivedanta Ashram and this is where my experience as a monk in New York began. The small apartment was on the top floor of a brownstone in the Lower East Side. It was cozy inside, with wooden floors and exposed brick walls. Pairs of monks shared the two larger bedrooms, which were just bigger than a suburban walk-in closet. The apartments below us were not affiliated with the ashram, and it took a little while for the other tenants to get used to seeing monks going in and out of their building. Some were open and friendly, but not everybody was thrilled to have us.

There were a total of five of us living at the Fourth Street place. This was my first experience in the States living a spiritual life. Even though I had explored my spirituality before going to India, I was still also working a corporate job. Now I had re-entered America as a completely different person. The entire time I was in India, I was pretty comfortable wearing robes. I wore white-colored robes because I hadn't made any commitments to the monastic order. Walking around New York City with robes and a buzzed haircut, I felt extremely self-conscious. It helped that I didn't have any friends or family in the area who could recognize me. This wasn't the case for one of our monks, who regularly ran into friends and family who wondered what had happened to him and why he was doing what he was doing.

Some tenants in the building knocked on our door complaining about the incense smell and the food that we were cooking. They said the smells were getting into their clothes. They also complained about the songs we would sing even though we tried to sing quite softly. Perhaps we weren't as quiet as we thought.

Sometimes, when it comes to religion and spirituality, people can be intolerant. This might be because they had some negative experiences in their own religious traditions, or it may be they were forced to go to church or a temple without wanting to go. Perhaps they were forced to engage in rituals without being given the proper explanation and meaning behind the ritual, or perhaps they were just made to feel guilty about not being more religious, being labeled as "sinners" because they weren't able to live up to the standards of their religious institutions. It is also completely possible that we weren't as mindful of our neighbors as we could have been.

Once, in an irritated and aggressive mood, one of our neighbors came into our apartment to tell us that we were making too much noise. Our head monk, who is six foot two inches tall and well built, escorted him out. The guy didn't protest in the moment, but later he returned to pound our front door with a hammer, leaving a huge dent. We were all really shocked that he would resort to such behavior.

In the culture of India, it is not uncommon to see monks walking on the streets, especially in holy places. They might stare at a young monk, but they would never become aggressive. Monks are respected in India and in some Asian cultures, and for the most part people in India understand that a monk hasn't given up engaging in the material world just to escape life, but that they've had some powerful epiphanies about life which have lead them down this path.

They might ask, "Why did you do this at such an early age?" "Why not live life, do your duty in the material world, and when you get older, give it all up?"

But this was America, and hearing comments such as "get a job" weren't unusual. Initially, I would become offended and even upset with these people, who were so quick to judge my life choices without knowing what I had been through. Over time, I learned not to take these things too seriously.

It can be easier to blend into the New York landscape. Here, it's not uncommon to see people of all ethnicities, religions, and cultures. Muslims and Hasidic Jews comfortably wear their traditional attire in public. There is even the occasional Buddhist monk, dressed in full-length robes and baring a shaved head. While I did not see many Hindu monks in white or orange saffron robes, I felt more at ease amidst other alternative cultures.

Then again, the streets are clogged with people and each moment is an opportunity to feel another's gaze. Moreover, I didn't have a vehicle and would either walk or take public transport everywhere. It took almost a full year for me to become comfortable wearing robes everywhere I went. It took a couple of years before I would actually feel confident about my lifestyle and my outward appearance.

LEARNING TO COOK

In addition to learning scripture and going deeper into our meditation, the monastic life encouraged self-sufficiency. Learning to cook was one of the first steps that pushed me in this direction. While growing up, my mom would cook for us on the weekends, but I never developed an interest in the kitchen or anything that had any relation to cooking. Even though my mom had been using Indian spices all of my life, I didn't recognize any of them. The only time I would go into the kitchen was after my mom had already cooked and the food was ready to be served. I think most Indian guys are raised this way. The only thing I could do in the kitchen was make toast and pour myself some cereal.

Communal life in the monastery required everyone to pull their weight with all services, including cooking. Here I was, 27-years-old, and I didn't even know how to peel, cut, or shred fruits and vegetables. It took me so long to do everything in the kitchen. It was all so foreign to me. Cutting vegetables took forever. I measured everything so precisely because I wasn't familiar with the spices and I wasn't aware how it would impact the whole preparation. I didn't really enjoy doing it, but intellectually, I knew it would be good for me to learn this skill, and I didn't have much choice. Little did I know how much this service was going to come in handy in the future when I would be called to teach cooking classes at Columbia University.

Things got tricky when I had to cook multiple things at once. It took some time and quite a few burnt preparations before I understood that I didn't need to always have the flame on high. After about six months to a year, when I finally started to get a handle on cooking, it began to feel like a liberating experience. I had always depended on friends, family, hosts, and restaurants to provide me with this essential commodity, but now I could do it on my own.

In the past, cooking had never been such a thoughtful process. I would just eat. I had developed a real relationship with my meal by searching out a recipe, shopping for it, cutting it up, cooking it, sharing it with others, and nourishing myself with it. As difficult as it was to learn, it was equally satisfying to acquire this valuable life tool.

LEARNING TO SING & PLAY INSTRUMENTS

I spent my first year in the Bhaktivedanta Ashram developing my musical skills. I never learned to play an instrument. When I was about nine years old, I got my parents to buy me a trumpet, but when we moved, I forgot to take it with me. Rhythms and melodies were not something that came easily to me. Actually, I was fairly tone-deaf.

Many of our spiritual practices and meditations involve singing and playing instruments. I was really uncomfortable when it was my turn to sing. I would sing off-pitch and couldn't keep the melody. That didn't help my confidence level, especially since I was living with monks who had a talent for music. A few years later, one of the monks told me that another monk had told him that when he had first heard me sing, he whispered "there's no hope for him." He was referring to my singing and not my devotional life.

I remember taking a choir class to complete my art requirements in 11th grade. Even though there were 50 of us in the class, when the teacher stopped to say someone was singing off-key, it was always me. I survived by lip-syncing. I never knew if I fooled my teacher with this routine, or if she just took pity on me when it came to grading.

At the monastery, I gradually learned to play the mridanga drum. It's a traditional oval-shaped, clay Bengali drum with two sides – one for the highs and one for the lows—and is worn around the neck so that it hangs down to one's belly. It took me about a year to get the basics down, probably about three times longer than it would take someone with some inclination for music. But I was determined to learn it. I got my drive to never give up from my father. He taught me that there wasn't anything I couldn't do and all I had to do was not give up. Gradually, I started playing along while the other monks sang and I even started playing at some of the temple gatherings. This was a definite confidence builder and tremendous breakthrough for me.

SPEAKING FROM THE SCRIPTURES

Each morning a monk would lecture from the scriptures. There were five of us and we would rotate lecturing. I was really impressed at everyone's ability

128

to read a passage and give a 30-minute talk without much preparation. Even during public programs, the monks, without much preparation, would very eloquently elaborate on the philosophy in an easily understandable manner.

To me, it was incomprehensible. I had turned down the offer to speak at our morning sessions, which was attended by three or four people. I was afraid I would forget what to say and would look like a total fool in front of the other monks. For most of my life, I had shied away from public speaking engagements, even to very small groups. Moreover, I didn't really have a very thorough understanding of the philosophy. I just barely knew the basics and it was definitely not enough to present in front of others. They already knew I was an inexperienced cook and a tone-deaf singer—I couldn't bear to imagine losing face at this as well!

However, I did know that I wouldn't be able to avoid this challenge for too much longer. I eventually agreed to speak. I was so nervous that I started preparation weeks in advance. I had accumulated pages and pages of notes of what I wanted to say, but I knew that there was no way I would be able to read or even really refer to them when I began to speak. My mind was racing and I had butterflies in my stomach. I reminded myself over and over that there were only four people in the room.

When I finally got up to speak, everything just flowed. No one was more surprised than I was. I had offered prayers to my teachers in my mind, and when I began speaking, all of the studying I had done started pouring out. I was able to communicate everything that I wanted to. I was so nervous during the process that my kurta (shirt) was soaked with perspiration. I realized that the prayers had worked. I still wasn't confident in my ability to speak publicly. I avoided it like the plague, but more and more situations would arise where I would need to speak about the philosophy, and I knew that I had to do it. Several years down the line, I was amazed to find that I was coming to enjoy speaking publicly.

Teaching is one of the most important duties of being a monk. Monks in many traditions become reclusive, distancing themselves from the general populace, but for monks within the bhakti or devotional tradition, the suggestion is to remain in cities and assist others in discovering their spirituality. We are encouraged to get involved in the lives of other people and perform the sacrifice of taking on other people's problems in order to lighten their load. We try to understand that compassion means to live selflessly by assisting others. Of course, not all monks are required to engage in this capacity, but it is encouraged. The reason that others and I take to the monastic order is to focus on our own spiritual progress, but this doesn't really happen until we learn to help others as much as we can. As the old adage goes "in giving we receive." I underwent a very serious transformation during my first year in the monastery. I was doing things I had never before done or thought to do and I was starting to enjoy it.

A SPLINTER IN THE MIND

I never imagined that I would be able to combine my newly discovered love of teaching with one of my favorite childhood pastimes: watching Hollywood movies. I didn't hear about *The Matrix* until five years after it was released in theatres. I had moved into the monastery the same year (1999) it was released and for the next five years, I had cut myself off from all television, movies, and even news. For the most part, I had lost all interest in things of this material world.

After hearing many people talk about the spiritual connections the movie had with Hindu philosophy, I finally decided to watch it in 2004. I was astonished to learn that the movie was suggesting that our present reality might just be illusory. I wondered how a movie was so accurately able to capture the state of mind of one on a spiritual quest and where they got the idea that our worldly existence is an illusion?

The only place I had come across these topics was in the *Bhagavad Gita*. I strongly related to the confused state of mind depicted by the character Neo. One of the first scenes of the movie shows him sleeping at his computer while searching for answers about the world he lives in. I recalled a section of the Gita which explains that we carry a false conception of ourselves because we identify with the physical body and aren't able to see or experience the soul. This specific teaching turned my paradigm of life upside down. I remember standing on the sidewalk and asking myself the question, is it possible that the self is different than the body? If so, wouldn't it mean, most of us are in some kind of illusion? Having my paradigm shifted and adjusting to a new one was hard and it took a while for me to adapt.

When Neo is finally rescued by Morpheus and the resistance and is shown what The Matrix really is, he refuses to believe that everything he ever believed was actually false and illusory. The experience is so intense for him that he throws up and falls unconscious. I never threw up or fell unconscious, but the paradigm shift did make me feel very confused and uneasy for some time because I no longer understood how I fit into society.

Besides beautifully capturing Neo's state of mind, the dialogue in the film is absolutely phenomenal. It begins with the exchange between Neo and Trinity where she suggests that we are being driven by "the question." There are so many questions that are driving us as humanity. When we're not keeping ourselves busy and distracted by all the gadgetry, I'm sure every human being has asked themselves the following questions:

- ❖ Who am I?
- ❖ What's my purpose in life?
- ❖ How did we all get here?

- ❖ Is there a God?
- ❖ Why is there suffering?
- ❖ Are we alone in the Universe or are there other beings out there?

Too quickly, life takes over, and we come to the conclusion that there may not be an answer to these questions. However, I don't think we can truly be satisfied until we at least attempt to answer these questions. They won't leave us alone.

Trinity goes on to suggest that the answer will find us if we want it to. It's possible for the answers to be right in front of our face, but if we're not looking for them, we will completely miss them. We keep ourselves so busy in life that we leave ourselves little or no time to explore the answers to these very profound questions. Society can almost make it seem like a waste of time to pursue these queries. The conversation dives even deeper when Neo and Morpheus finally meet. Morpheus challenges Neo to explore the difference between reality and illusion. Chapter two in the Gita separates the body and soul:

> *As a person puts on new garments, giving up old ones, the soul similarly accepts new material bodies, giving up the old and useless ones.*

Chapter eight of the Gita marks another distinction between the illusory world of matter and the spiritual world.

> *Yet there is another unmanifest nature, which is eternal and is transcendental to this manifested and unmanifested matter. It is supreme and is never annihilated. When all in this world is annihilated, that part remains as it is.*

The concept of "guru" or spiritual teacher is wonderfully depicted through the interaction of Morpheus and Neo. It parallels the interaction between Krishna and Arjuna in the Gita. Just as Arjuna inquires from Krishna about his purpose in life, Neo is asking about the real world as distinct from the matrix.

Krishna and Morpheus both make it clear to their disciples that they can exercise their free will to either accept the advice or reject it, a theme that recurs at every major turn in *The Matrix*. This is true of every spiritual seeker. At each moment, at each stage of our progress, we decide how far we want to go and we can be sure that many tests and temptations will come to distract us from our spiritual pursuits.

RELIGIOUS HARMONY

I learned from my conversations with New Yorkers on the street and students in the local universities that they were very wary of religious people professing that their faith was the only true way to God. A very common question I was often asked and am still asked today is, "Do you think your truth is the only truth, or do you feel other traditions also offer a valid truth?" From my experience, those who claim to have the only truth haven't taken the time to study other teachings or are just close-minded. I am confident that if we made even a slight endeavor to understand another's faith, it would make all the difference in the world.

The first time I watched *Jesus of Nazareth* with a group of fellow Hindu monks, we marveled at the life of Jesus and the seriousness of his teachings. We felt immediately that we could find similar teachings in our own tradition. The video inspired me to read the Gospels, which surprised me even more. The mood of a religious practitioner described by Jesus is identical to descriptions in the *Gita* and the *Bhagavat Purana*.

> *You have heard the law that says, 'Love your neighbor' and hate your enemy. But I say, love your enemies! Pray for those who persecute you! In that way, you will be acting as true children of your Father in heaven.* (Matthew 5:43-45)

135

The Dalai Lama teaches us that the purpose of religion from the Buddhist perspective "is to facilitate love, compassion, tolerance, humility, and forgiveness." In the 13th chapter of the *Bhagavad Gita*, Krishna gives items of knowledge that can help liberate the soul, *"Humility; nonviolence; tolerance; simplicity...all these I declare to be knowledge..."*

The *Bhagavat Purana* is full of stories of individuals who were ready to forgive the perpetrator for even the most grievous offenses. It teaches us that if we learn to forgive others, God will also forgive us. Finding such similarities between these traditions was quite exciting, as I realized that the message of God is similar across seemingly different traditions.

In order to understand this, we first need to acknowledge that God must have given messages of liberation and salvation to people throughout the world. God wasn't partial when He distributed spiritual knowledge. We need to give up our sectarian views and abandon the thought that only the people of a certain tradition have been blessed and that all others have been condemned. I don't think there is anything that turns people away from religion and spirituality more than this kind of an attitude. Even if someone is curious about spiritual truths and practices, a fanatic and sectarian practitioner can drive him or her away.

While all traditions share some similar tenets, not all religions are the same. Different practices, philosophies, and theologies will reach different types of people. I don't necessarily have to agree with the teachings of other traditions in order to respect them. Too often we feel insecure because we're not grounded in our own tradition, and the only way to overcome that insecurity is to fanatically push our religious teachings onto others.

I remember a Hindu monk saying during a lecture that just as a dog can always recognize its owner, whether the owner is dressed in shorts, a suit, or nothing at all, so a mature spiritualist is able to recognize his or her God in the dress of another tradition. I know from personal experience that this is easier said than done, but if we don't at least attempt to move in this direction, then we'll continue to fight over who's right and who's wrong. Because the tradition we have chosen is having such an amazing impact on our lives, we may feel inclined to express to the world that it's the best. However, it's important to acknowledge that the tradition one has chosen may be best for that individual but not the best path for everyone else on the planet. All spheres of life are full of varieties and different people are attracted to the different gifts life has to offer. So why can't we see the varieties of spiritual paths as part of the variety of gifts offered to us by the Divine and be happy with our choice and let others be happy with their choices?

9/11

Towards the end of my second year at the monastery, I decided to take a short break from the city and visit a retreat center in West Virginia. Since it was a full 12-hour ride, I wanted to start early and decided to take the 8:00 a.m. bus from Port Authority in New York City. About an hour into the ride, I could see the bus driver in a semi-panicked mood communicating with someone through the bus radio. A short while later, the bus stopped somewhere in the outskirts of Pennsylvania and we were told we could go outside and stretch our legs. Most of us took him up on his offer and stepped outside.

After we got back in, the driver announced, "we will be stopping at the next bus station and all bus service, nationwide, is being suspended and no further information is available."

The announcement, in addition to his strange behavior, worried me. I felt anxious that he would drop us off at the next stop, in the middle of nowhere. We eventually stopped at a bus depot just outside of Harrisburg, Pennsylvania. I went to the customer service counter and asked why the bus had stopped and when service would resume. They told me that some kind of hijacking had taken place but that they didn't have any further details. Restless passengers from a few buses were waiting around trying to figure out what was going on. I called a friend who knew someone in Harrisburg and asked him to come pick me up. The acquaintance arrived driving a pickup truck. I got in, thanked him for picking me up, and immediately asked him if he knew what was happening.

"The World Trade Center came down," he said.

"You mean it got bombed?" I clarified.

"No, it got hit by a plane and it came down," he explained.

I was in total disbelief that a building that size could completely collapse. I asked if he was serious. Instead of responding for a third time, he flipped on the radio. I couldn't believe it even after I had heard it with my own ears. The twin towers had been hit by two different planes within about 15 minutes and had crumbled to the ground, leaving nothing standing.

Because I lived near downtown, the towers were an iconic part of my New York life. Every once in a while I'd walk around the World Trade Center, sometimes alone and sometimes with friends, and would stop to stare at those towers in amazement. A couple of years prior to their destruction, I had taken some friends visiting from Los Angeles to the top of the towers. Those towers were the pride and joy of New York's skyline.

Even after hearing the news, I had a hard time believing that they had been obliterated until I saw pictures. When I saw a video replay of the horrific event, my stomach churned in disgust. It was unbelievable that an attack this blatant and aggressive could take place right in our backyard. Smashing planes into buildings! What kind of an individual would think something like that up and have the ability and resources to carry it through to completion?

I didn't get back into New York City for almost a month after 9/11 and missed the immediate impact the event had on everyone. By the time I returned, the confusion and panic had died down. Eventually, I learned that religious extremists were behind this terrible act of violence.

It's unfortunate that so much of the world's violence gets tied to religion. Just because some misguided individuals fanatically and aggressively interpret their religious teachings, all of religion develops a bad reputation. Many people want to remove religion altogether because of the violence linked to it. However, while it's true much of the violence in our history was in the name of creed, religion isn't promoting violence. On the contrary, the actions of Gandhi, Martin Luther King, Jr., Mother Teresa, and many others, demonstrate that religion promotes tolerance, forgiveness, compassion, and selfless service to others. The real problem is that people can take spiritual teachings completely out of context and use certain passages to justify their misdeeds.

This happens within all traditions to some degree or another. For example, some members of the Hindu community will overly simplify Hinduism by stating that, "it says to do your duty and don't hurt others."

While it's true that Hinduism suggests this, it has many more teachings that go along with this message to make it complete. It also tells us to spend time worshipping God, studying scriptures, and serving humanity.

Pulling out just one part of the message is like utilizing only a portion of the directions to get to your destination while disregarding the rest. How far will we get and how much sense is it going to make? People have a tendency to find something, anything from spiritual texts that they are able to apply into their lives and treat that as the all-in-all. While it's all right to apply whatever one is capable of practicing, one should carefully understand the teachings in their proper context so that they are not misapplied, which could lead to fanaticism.

CHAPTER NINE

THE HEART OF YOGA COME WEST

The strand of Hinduism that I began to practice in New York before I went to India, and that I continued to practice while staying in the Mumbai and New York monasteries, is known as Gaudiya Vaishnavism. Many people in the Western world know this as the Hare Krishna movement. Bhaktivedanta Swami Prabhupada brought it to the West. He was born in Calcutta in 1896 in a traditional Hindu Bengali family. He was very spiritual in his early youth, but had developed a suspicion of "holy men" in young adulthood. His father would constantly invite holy men called "sadhus" over to his home to ask for their blessings; but when he saw them smoking and drinking afterwards, he began to doubt their motivation.

In 1922, a friend of his insisted that he accompany him to a lecture being delivered by a spiritual teacher, Srila Bhaktisiddhanta Sarasvati. Prabhupada, then known as Abhay, told his friend he didn't want to listen to another teacher whose character may be doubtful. However, at the insistence of his friend, Prabhupada went along. They arrived and offered their respects to the teacher, as is customary within India. The teacher immediately told them that they looked like educated young men and that they should take these spiritual teaching of India to the West. Prabhupada was surprised. After all, this was the first time he was seeing this teacher and without even getting to know him, the teacher was offering a fairly substantial instruction, even a life's mission. Prabhupada felt in his heart a certain genuineness about the teacher and the conviction with which he had spoken. After the meeting, he accepted Bhaktisiddhanta as his teacher. He kept the original instruction within his heart and mind, but it wasn't until 1965, a full 28 years after the passing away of Bhaktisiddhanta, that Prabhupada would be able to follow through on this instruction.

It was at the ripe old age of 69 that Prabhupada decided to leave the shores of India and venture out to America to bring the teachings of Gaudiya Vaishnavism to the Western world. He had never left India before and he didn't know anyone in America. He journeyed to the United States on a cargo ship and the voyage took one full month. He experienced tremendous difficulty on the trip—seasickness, nausea, and even two heart attacks. He turned seventy on the ship. The ship first stopped in Boston harbor for a couple of days and then sailed to New York.

When he finally landed in New York, he didn't know whether to turn left or right. There was no one to see him off when he left India, and no one to greet him when he landed in America. He had only seven rupees with him, and no dollars. Despite these setbacks, from 1965 to 1977, he miraculously managed to start over 100 temples worldwide and translate and comment on over 50 volumes of Hindu scriptures. He traveled around the world a dozen times, and developed an international following of over 5,000 disciples.

This was the first time in the history of Hinduism that a large scale number of non-Hindus—Americans, Europeans, Africans, South Americans, and Asians—were adopting into their everyday lives the philosophy, ritual, and practices of ancient Hinduism. As far as I know, this was the first time within Hinduism that Indian and Western women were becoming priests and engaging in service on the altar. Prabhupada established the International Society for Krishna Consciousness in New York City in 1966.

Prabhupada met the Beatles through his London disciples, who had started their own center there. The disciples invited Prabhupada to come to London to meet the famous pop band, hopeful that through this connection they could expand the movement. When Prabhupada arrived at the airport, his disciples had arranged for a team of reporters to be there ready to interview him. After the airport interviews, he was driven to John Lennon's estate. There he got to meet John Lennon, George Harrison, and Yoko Ono. Of the three, George felt the strongest connection to Prabhupada. He even went on to write the hit song *My Sweet Lord* dedicated to the deity Krishna. In the background vocals, the Hare Krishna mantra can be heard.

Allen Ginsberg, the famous American poet of the Beat Generation, was another prominent personality of the time who took an interest in Prabhupada's work. Ginsberg would visit Prabhupada at his Second Avenue temple on the Lower East Side. Ginsberg later toured with Prabhupada to help promote his cause. Although Ginsberg didn't become a follower or disciple, he greatly appreciated the work that Prabhupada was doing.

People of all backgrounds – hippies, students, and working folks – were becoming disciples of Prabhupada. One of his more prominent disciples was the great grandson of Henry Ford. Alfred Ford helped Prabhupada to acquire the Fisher mansion in Detroit and continued to provide tremendous financial assistance to the growing Krishna society.

When Prabhupada had arrived in the 1960s, America was experiencing division over the Vietnam War and the civil rights movement. Most of Prabhupada's early followers were part of a counterculture, which had rejected conservative American culture and opposed our participation in the Vietnam War.

Because a large part of the practice involved the chanting of the Hare Krishna mantra, it became known to the Western world as the Hare Krishna movement.

THE PROPHET SHRI CHAITANYA

The Hare Krishna movement is a part of Hinduism. Its official name is Gaudiya Vaisnavism. Gaudiya refers to the region of India presently known as Bengal; Vaisnava refers to one who worships the deity Vishnu or Krishna. At least half of the Hindu population would consider themselves Vaisnavas. So, basically, the Hare Krishnas are worshippers of Krishna from the Bengal region.

The first proponent of the tradition was Shri Chaitanya (1486-1534) who was born in West Bengal. He is depicted in paintings as tall and slim with a golden complexion and long black hair. His look probably appealed to the hippies of the 60s. One could say he looks like Jesus without the beard and mustache. Before adopting monkhood, he would take groups of devotees from his area in Western Bengal into the village with musical instruments and chant the names of Krishna. At 24, he left home, became a monk and for the next several years traveled like a mendicant throughout India encouraging people to chant the names of God. He explained that whoever chants the name of God will achieve cleansing of the heart. Further, anyone who hears the names of God will also achieve purification of the heart. Thus, he encouraged his followers to chant in public so everyone could benefit from hearing the names of God. For the last 18 years of his life, he settled in

Jagannath Puri, which is located in the Eastern part of India in the state of Orissa. His mother was a widow and had requested him to stay in Jagannath Puri, a city not too far from where she lived so she could continue to get news about him.

He didn't introduce anything that wasn't already part of ancient Hindu culture. Rather, he chose to emphasize certain teachings and practices from within Hinduism. First and foremost, he emphasized the preeminence of Krishna's position over the other gods and stressed that Krishna possesses a form and personality, which is not subject to human fallibility. In addition to citing scripture to verify his claim, he explained that Krishna is God who wants his devotees to love him without fear. Chaitanya further explained that the highest goal a devotee can achieve is to serve and befriend Krishna eternally upon achieving the spiritual realm.

KRISHNA

Krishna wore many hats: child, friend, servant, romantic lover, cowherd boy, and killer of demons. For someone coming from a Western paradigm—and even for some Hindus—Krishna can easily be passed off as a mythological figure, similar to Greek or Norse gods, now only suitable for comic books.

However, hundreds of millions of people undertake severe fasts, engage in extended rituals and worship, recite extensively his activities and the verses of the *Bhagavad Gita* for the purpose of remembering him and his deeds. His appearance is calculated according to the lunar calendar and is usually in mid-August. Krishna's life is studied in university courses on Hinduism and debated by philosophers and theologians all over the world. Those who are unfamiliar with his life and activities are befuddled by Krishna, but devotees rejoice upon hearing and reading the wonderful stories of his life.

One of the most endearing qualities demonstrated by Krishna, during his presence on earth, was his willingness to interact with his devotees in a variety of relationships. Even though he is the supreme deity according to the *Gita* and some of the *Puranas* (ancient histories), he always experiences great joy in the service of his devotees. As a child, he would carry his father's shoes on his head and bring them to his father. Similar to Jesus washing the feet of his twelve disciples at the last supper, Krishna, with great joy, washed the feet of great saintly persons. His most prominent act of service happened immediately after he spoke the *Gita*, when he drove Arjuna on his chariot for 18 days like a humble chauffeur. The entire time, he obeyed every order of Arjuna like a servant. Krishna didn't hesitate to change his role from friend, to teacher, to servant. These descriptions of Krishna's activities can be very difficult to comprehend, especially if one is used to the notion of a God being the supreme father who is angry, jealous, and eager to punish those who don't follow his law. Krishna is none of these things. Rather, he can be described as a poet, a singer, dancer, and servant. All one has to do is look at a sunset, sunrise, or any of the other wonders of nature to understand the creative and artistic side of Krishna.

As I began to learn about Krishna, I was intrigued by the description given in the ancient Hindu text, the *Brahma Samhita*: "*He has an eternal blissful spiritual body...He is a person possessing the beauty of a blooming youth...*" In other words, God is not an old man with a long white beard. I found this to be a very refreshing idea! If God was old, it meant he would be affected by time and subject to decay and possibly even death. Here he's described as an eternally youthful person beyond time and space. It's not possible for us, with our limited and inaccurate sense perception and logic, to comprehend the nature, quality, and personhood of Krishna. Hindu scriptures and sages explain that one needs to qualify oneself by purifying one's senses, mind, and consciousness in order to understand God. Purifying one's senses, mind, consciousness, and soul is the prerequisite for gaining access to this knowledge. For example, before studying calculus, one needs to qualify oneself by studying arithmetic, algebra, and geometry; otherwise, calculus doesn't make any sense. In order to approach God, qualities of pride, envy, greed, anger, and selfish desire must be purged since they cloud the ego. Simultaneously, humility, non-violence, forgiveness, and tolerance need to be implemented into our character in order to bring clarity into our lives. Without endeavoring to fulfill these prerequisites, God will only remain a theoretical concept.

Getting to know Krishna is a lot like getting to know anyone: it requires time and commitment. Krishna explains in the *Gita* that he doesn't need or want anything from anyone, but one who renders service to him becomes his friend. All in all, even though he's the supreme creator and the cause of all causes, he's looking to engage in a loving reciprocal relationship with those who are interested and he promises that it will be a two-way street where he's willing to do his part. He constantly sends people or messages into our lives, which will bring us closer to Him.

A beautiful connection rewards those willing to undergo the process of purifying one's mind and senses. One can come face to face with the supreme and engage in a loving relationship with him. In that relationship, one can be a servant, friend, parent, or a lover of Krishna. Each relationship is unique and has its own flavor, and whatever relationship one achieves with Krishna is completely satisfying for that individual. It is explained in the spiritual texts that the greatest intimacy with Krishna exists in the relationship of a lover as it includes the qualities of friendship and service. Even in this material world, the deepest relationship exists between two lovers. One then enters into an eternal relationship residing in the spiritual realm with God and unlimited spiritual beings all of whom share the desire to render selfless service to the Divine and to each other.

PURIFYING THE HEART OF ENVY, PRIDE, GREED, AND ANGER

Revelation of the divine doesn't necessarily happen within one lifetime, as the full process of purification can take multiple lives. The encouraging part is that to the degree envy, anger, greed, and pride start to diminish, to that degree we start experiencing the presence of the Divine in nature, in ourselves, and in others around us. The negative qualities are within our hearts and minds and can be compared to a tree with extremely deep roots. The problem is that we don't even recognize that we have them or how deeply rooted they are.

We can probably all relate to a time when we hoped to acquire or achieve something and someone else got it. We start feeling envious and hope their success falls through somehow. We might even go so far as to sabotage another's project because of the envy. We start comparing ourselves to them and find ways in which we are superior to them. The mind starts finding all kinds of faults in their character, and even if they're really just a projection of our consciousness onto them, the mind can dwell on them for days, week, months, or even years, depending on the magnitude of the event. The recommendation, which is a very difficult one, is to accept what happened and to be happy for the other person's success. Being happy for another's success, especially if we were competing with them is practically impossible! However, if we are aspiring for eternal residence with the Divine, then we need to come to this platform. That is a prerequisite for attaining the goal because in the spiritual realm, envy doesn't exist.

PRIDE

Pride is a quality that is deeply buried within our hearts. Our achievements cause us to feel superior to others and inflate our ego. We don't hesitate to take full credit for things achieved, but often forget that all of our abilities and talents are coming from God and can be taken away at any time. In many cases, we lose sight of our passion for our work and are instead driven by the desire to outdo someone else and therefore prove to them and everyone else that "I'm better." This tendency is there when we're children and remains with us lifetime after lifetime.

Queen Kunti, the mother of Arjuna, explains that one cannot pray with sincere feelings if one's heart is contaminated with pride because the proper mood in prayer can't be evoked if one is feeling superior to others. Many other spiritual teachers also warn of the dangers of a prideful heart. As monks, we're supposed to live lives of simplicity and humility, but even for us it's very challenging to maintain these ideas when people begin to glorify and praise us for our renunciation or our lectures. Offering respect to monks is a common custom in India and one way this is expressed is by touching the feet of holy men or monks. I was very uncomfortable when this started happening to me shortly after moving into the monastery. People approached me after lectures to touch my feet or sometimes simply because I was wearing robes. I didn't consider myself a "holy man" because I knew that many unholy tendencies were lingering in my heart. The more I insisted that they not touch my feet, the more they thought I was being humble and this would increase their enthusiasm for touching my feet. It was a no-win situation. At a certain point, I just stopped trying. It's very hard to not let something like this get to your head because the ego wants to feel superior to others. On many occasions, I would allow my ego to get inflated by feeling that I was better in some way or another from everyone else, but deep down inside I would try and remind myself that this feeling would be very detrimental to my spiritual life.

GREED

Greed stems from dissatisfaction with what one already has. Once such discontent stirs, it cannot be satisfied by the material possession it feasts upon. Globally, this has become a major issue. Practically every type of industry is exploiting and polluting the planet to make as much profit as possible simply due to greed. Even though a lot of corporations know the damage they're causing to the health of people with their businesses, greed for money prevents them from stopping or even slowing down their activities.

When we get everything we want, we want to have more than the next person. If we get a million dollars, we need ten million, and if we get that, we need one hundred million. It just goes on. There is no satiation point. It's like a fire: the more fuel we put into it, the more it grows. Money and things will never pacify greed; it can only drive us mad and make us lose sight of ourselves and the consequences of our actions. Some will go so far as to break the law to satisfy their greed, even if they already had more money than they could spend and more properties than they could use.

ANGER

Anger creates rifts between friends and even the closest of relatives. Throughout human history, anger has led to wars between nations. The second chapter of the *Bhagavad Gita* explains that anger has the potential to switch off our intelligence and thus causes us to become unaware of what is right and what is wrong. In the blind rage of anger, we end up saying and doing things that can cause tremendous emotional, psychological, and physical pain upon others. Friendships can be destroyed and families can fall apart. It leads us to engage in actions we end up regretting our entire lives.

Chaitanya introduced some very revolutionary ideas. He very openly opposed the idea that one's caste or position in society could disqualify one from engaging in certain temple rituals. He insisted that external designations didn't matter when it came to worshiping God and making spiritual advancement. Traditionally, in order for one to be able to perform rituals in the temple, one had to be born in a family of priests. Chaitanya wanted to emphasize that if one has the inclination towards spiritual pursuits, then they shouldn't be prevented based on their birth. Prabhupada carried this same attitude of acceptance forward when he came to the West.

The Hare Krishna movement has very interesting, one can say even very strange, beginnings. It is always fascinating me to imagine someone like Prabhupada, who grew up in a very conservative culture in India in the early 1900s, interacting with young American hippies who lived by the motto "sex, drugs, and rock n' roll." Prabhupada was raised in an environment where he never ate meat, never drank alcohol, and never smoked.

He used to give lectures on the *Bhagavad Gita* from a storefront on Second Avenue three times a week—Monday, Wednesday, and Friday. Chanting the Hare Krishna mantra, which was accompanied by a variety of instruments, would follow the lectures. Some (maybe even most) of the people who attended his lectures did drugs before arriving, so it's hard to say how much they understood of what he was trying to explain, especially through his thick Indian accent. Even I had a hard time understanding him when I first listened to one of his recorded lectures, and I grew up with Indian parents who speak with an Indian accent.

He would personally cook traditional Indian food for the 20 or 30 guests that would come, and afterwards clean up all the cooking utensils and plates. Most of the time, he would do it all by himself. It wasn't until quite some time later that it occurred to some of them that they should stick around to help clean up the place. Initially, he wasn't attracting the most responsible group of people, but he was happy serving them because he knew that he was fulfilling his spiritual teacher's wish for him to come West to teach and serve.

He left the Lower East Side of New York and went to the other hub of the hippie culture, the Haight Asbury district in Northern California to open a second center. His third would eventually open in Los Angeles, a center I remember seeing when I was a kid. When I saw the Hare Krishnas singing and dancing on the streets of Los Angeles, I used to think that it's fine if they want to sing in dance, but they should do it inside, not out in public. It definitely didn't look like anything I wanted to be a part of.

My father traveled to and from America in the late 60s and early 70s for business, well before our family moved there, so his first encounter with a Hare Krishna monk was at the Chicago airport where a monk approached him and tried to sell him a book. My father saw that he was being sold a *Bhagavad Gita* and felt happy to see that this monk was trying to spread Hindu teachings. My dad gave him a $20 bill and said that he could give the book to someone else.

In the 60s and 70s, no one could really figure out what the movement was all about. Even many who joined didn't really understand what it was. Some liked it because it involved the chanting of Indian mantras. Some liked the fact that you could dance as part of the worship. Perhaps some liked it because of the incense or a combination of all of these exotic Indian things. Many were attracted by the amazing vegetarian food; others by the philosophy. Most were confused about the origins of the movement. Witnessing Western men with shaved heads, wearing saffron-colored bed sheets, bearing vertical yellow markings on their foreheads, singing and dancing on the streets while playing Indian instruments, was an unusual sight. In the first few years of the movement, before they were able to obtain traditional cloth from India, the members actually wore bed sheets. This was the first time anyone had seen American women wearing traditional Indian saris chanting and dancing on the streets. This was a strange sight even for the 60s.

The movement looked as confusing to the Americans as it did to the Indians. Americans couldn't relate to this phenomenon. Everything about the tradition was strange to them—the attire, the music, the incense, and the philosophy. Indian people in America recognized the tradition, except that very young white people were doing everything they've always seen older brown people do in India. The clothing was familiar because within Hinduism, holy persons wear dhotis, long pieces of cloth in white or saffron, that wrap around the lower portion of the body and another cloth that covers the upper portion. The dhoti represents simplicity. It's plain cloth without a fancy or elaborate design and the idea is that we want to be simple before God. Up until this day, my grandfather in India wears a dhoti all day long. It was also the cloth of choice for Gandhi, and the traditional cloth of pre-colonial India.

Indians would have also recognized the shaved head, a sign of renunciation within the Hindu tradition for many of the monks, and of course, they were also very familiar with the Hare Krishna mantra. I think the thing that threw them off was the Western people and the dancing, which is practiced by only a few sections of Hinduism. When I first went to the temple in New York while still working as a loan officer, this is the thing I found to be most distracting. Here I am trying to meditate, pray, and chant with my heart and soul, and meanwhile here are the regulars jumping up and down in ecstasy because the rhythm of the chanting is escalating and the drums are increasing in numbers and volume. It took me a really long time to get comfortable with it and even longer to participate in it.

Since there were hardly any Hindu temples in America in the 60s and 70s, most Hindus would go to the Hare Krishna temples opened by Prabhupada and his followers. His temples became the main places of worship for Hindus in the 60s, 70s, and continued on to the 80s. Gradually, as more Hindus migrated into the country, more Hindu temples started popping up around the country, giving the Hindu population a greater choice. For many Hindus, they felt more comfortable being in a temple where Indians performed the rituals and where there were multiple deities.

The demographics have shifted dramatically within the Krishna temples. It has changed from mostly members of the Western counterculture to a majority working professionals of Indian origin, including engineers, doctors, business people, teachers, and all other walks of life. Most temples within North America have a congregation that is made up of at least 80 percent Indians. It's hard to put a finger on why this has happened. Some within the movement say that times have changed and that the movement was successful because of the counterculture. Others say the commitments to avoiding meat, alcohol, gambling, and premarital sex are too rigid for the Western lifestyle. It could also be the simple fact that there are a lot more Hindus in the country. Perhaps, it's a combination of all the above. At present, the movement has temples, restaurants, and farm communities in most major countries. It is doing extremely well in India and is flourishing in some of the former Eastern block countries.

Even if people didn't understand or like other aspects of the culture, everyone agreed that the food was awesome! I felt like I was addicted to it. It was Indian food, stuff that I had eaten all my life, but something was different and I couldn't figure it out. After a long week of work, I would eagerly wait for Sunday evening to arrive. Even though I enjoyed chanting and lecture portions of the program, I couldn't wait to get my hands on the food. In fact, I'd start thinking about it mid-week while sitting at my desk at work. The preparation that drove me completely nuts was the dessert. It was called halava, a very traditional Indian preparation made in temples in India for visitors and by families on special religious holidays. I had eaten halava many times, but this halava was out of this world. I'd stuff myself silly all the while wondering why I was hooked on the food, especially the halava. I just couldn't figure it out. It's a very simple preparation to make: you melt some butter or ghee (clarified butter), add some farina or cream of wheat, cook it for some time, and throw in some boiling hot water with sugar. That was it. So why was I, like many others, coming back again and again for food that I could have easily made at home? What was special about it?

The only difference was that this food was sanctified because it had been offered to Krishna. But I didn't think this would affect the taste. I later learned that when food is offered to Krishna, Krishna tastes the food and since the food comes in touch with divinity, the quality and taste change. I kind of believed it, but still wasn't sure how it really worked until I started teaching cooking classes at Columbia University. Students to this day come up to me with the same excitement about the food that I had when I first started eating sanctified food. Not only would they gobble down the halava, they brought Tupperware and would pack it up and take it back to their dorms. Seeing so many of them having the same response to the food as me, I became a believer in the power of offering food and its inherent connection to the divine that it brings about.

Also familiar to the Hindu community were the rituals being performed in the temple to worship Radha and Krishna, feminine and masculine aspects of God, which included incense, a flame, water, a flower, and a peacock fan. This ceremony is referred to as *arti*. The idea behind using all of these items to worship God is that we're offering back to God some of the most precious ingredients of this world, water and fire, without which we would not be able to survive. There isn't much that we can really offer to God, so we're just offering back parts of what God has given us. It's like a child might purchase a gift for his or her parents using allowance money; it may seem pointless, but it is the thoughtfulness of the child that matters to the parents. So, too, are our offerings to

God measured by our intentions and our mindfulness, not the material itself.

The two major texts taught in the Krishna temples were ones that most Hindus probably had a copy of in their homes growing up. These texts were the *Bhagavad Gita* and the *Bhagavat Purana*. Growing up in Los Angeles, I had copies of both texts on my bookshelf. Of course, I would only glance at them because they seemed really interesting, but the moment I saw Sanskrit or tried to actually understand the philosophy, I would promptly close the book and return it to its place on the shelf. Even though it was translated into English, the Sanskrit made the philosophy feel intimidating and irrelevant. My situation is very similar to that of most Hindus I come across. The majority of the Hindus I talk to about the *Gita* know a verse or two from it, but hardly anyone has actually read it cover to cover. I'm assuming the same situation is true for people of other faiths in relation to their own scriptures. For Hindus, the *Bhagavad Gita* is as prominent a text as the bible is for Christians. There was a time in India where participants in court proceedings would be required to swear on the Gita that they would tell the truth. The Gita is the most commented on Hindu text. There are over 500 commentaries. It may even be the most commented on spiritual text of all time. It's considered a practical guide to everyday living and it covers topics that encourage one to introspect about the nature and deeper purpose to life. The Krishna tradition, however, stood apart from the rest of Hinduism because of its strict adherence to monotheism. Within Hinduism, there are millions of gods and most Hindus offer prayers and devotion to more than one. One of the most popular ones is Ganesh, the elephant god who removes obstacles in one's life. Then there's Laxmi, the goddess of wealth, and Sarasvati, the goddess who bestows knowledge upon the worshipper. Siva is one of the most prominent gods, and is always seen sitting in meditation with a cobra wrapped around his neck. He is considered by many to be the most powerful deity and people will pray to him for a whole variety of things such as protection, mystic powers, etc. Women pray to him for a good husband. The Krishna tradition, however, focuses all of its worship on Krishna and is therefore considered a monotheistic faith. Since the essential text is the *Gita*, and this text states that Krishna is the supreme creator of the spiritual and material worlds, the Krishna folks focused all of their energy on Krishna. Some Hindus felt uncomfortable with a single deity and felt that they were neglecting the other gods. This caused many of them to start visiting other temples that were being established which had multiple altars for the various deities.

Ever since my family came to America, we had a small altar with pictures of about 10 gods. Every morning, my parents would clean the pictures on the altar, light and offer an incense, offer a flower to each of the gods and then begin praying by chanting mantras. Following in their footsteps, I would also engage myself in the daily ritual, which I enjoyed. I definitely felt a certain satisfaction from the daily worship.

THE GODS

Why the Hindus worship so many gods and goddesses is a real mystery for most people. In the West, where the majority of people are part of the Abrahamic faith tradition that follows one God, the concept of polytheism is nothing more than fantasy or mythology worthy of comic book material. The interesting thing is that while Westerners can see it as fiction, Hindus, without a second thought, can walk into a temple with multiple deities, bow down and offer prayer and worship with devotion, treating that deity as much like a person as you and me. There is one logical way to understand this complicated theology of millions of gods according to the Gaudiya Vaisnava tradition: for a country, state, or city to run properly, the government creates various departments and employs individuals within those departments: teachers, postal workers, police and military personnel, construction works, doctors, politicians, and so many more. Each of these departments employs hundreds or thousands of individuals carrying out their respective duties. Each sector has one or more individuals who oversee the activities of that one department. Each head of an area is endowed with certain privileges and powers, which facilitates them in their tasks. It's probably safe to say that the number of individuals working for the United States government goes into the millions. This is just to keep one country working. Multiply that by all the countries on the planet, which is around 200, and all the people working for these governments, the total would easily come out to tens of millions of people employed by the various governments of the world. In order to keep the whole universe running, Krishna has put into place individuals that oversee the different parts of the material universe. These individuals are powerful beings that have been appointed by Krishna and have been bestowed with the necessary powers and abilities to manage and govern their part of creation. We call them gods. For example, the god responsible for the sun is called Surya. There is another person responsible for the moon. There are individuals overseeing the oceans, the wind, and practically every facet of creation. When seen from this perspective, 330 million is not that big a number.

We take it completely for granted that the sun is always perfectly fixed in its position. If it were to move even slightly closer to the earth we would burn to a crisp, but if it were to distance itself from us, we would become popsicles. We also take it for granted that all day and all night, there is air in the atmosphere for us to breathe. It's not by chance that all of this exists. It has been placed here and someone has been put in charge of each aspect of it. For example, when we plug our electronic gadgetry into power outlets, it's not by chance that it works. It was constructed into the building to facilitate our needs. If for some reason there's a massive power outage, then the person in charge would have to take responsibility for its maintenance. The material universe is functioning like a big governmental structure with heads of departments managing their respective affairs. These heads or "demigods" have also been endowed with abilities to confer benediction upon humanity, and that's why so many people pray to the different gods to have their material wishes fulfilled.

According to the scriptures, the gods live in different realms with life spans that are much longer than ours. For example, when six months pass here on earth, only one day goes by in the upper realms. Another six months equals one night. When a full day goes by for them, a full year has passed here on earth. According to human calculation, their lives span up to several billion years. This may sound quite fantastic to one who is hearing it for the first time, but it's actually not very different than what Einstein said about the relativity of time. Einstein's hypothetical experiment known as the "twin paradox" suggests that if one of a pair of twins travels into outer space at the speed of light, while the other remains on earth, when the space traveling twin returns, he will be younger than his counterpart on earth.

There is also a story from the ancient Puranas, which parallels Einstein's hypothetical experiment. By the power of his trained mind, a yogi exited the earthly realm for the higher planetary realms. When he arrived, the inhabitants of these higher realms told him that millions of years had instantly passed on Earth in the mere moments since he had entered the higher realms. The understanding that time is relative is nothing new for the Hindu tradition. It was quite common knowledge for most Hindus. After their allotted span of time, they die, and then different living beings are placed into those positions to continue overseeing their duties. This is similar to any governmental post. Each person in that post serves for a certain duration and then is replaced. It's not an eternal post. I'm trying to keep the explanation somewhat simple, as it's a bit more complicated.

There are also realms that go beyond the heavenly sphere. The highest realm within the material cosmos is Satyaloka, where Brahma resides. His entire life span, if calculated in terms of human years, is 311 trillion years. To him, it just feels like 100 years. Brahma takes birth from the naval of Vishnu, a manifestation of Krishna, and is given the task of creating the material universes within which lies the Earth. The material universe has the same life span as Brahma and is temporary, while the spiritual world, where Krishna resides, is eternal. Brahma overseas everything within the material sphere, including all godly beings. After his allotted life span, he also has to die. The conclusion is that nothing in the material world is permanent. From his perspective of time, our existence is similar to that of bacteria or some kind of microorganism. There are some organisms that only live for a few minutes or a few hours, but for that organism, it was a full and complete life. From our human perspective, it was just a blink of an eye.

CHAPTER TEN
SOUL FOOD AT COLUMBIA

Within the first year and a half of my life in the monastery, I was invited by a friend to come up to Albany and lecture on the *Bhagavad Gita* to a small group of Indian graduate students at his home. Although I was more than a little nervous to speak in front of such successful young people, I knew that it was my duty as a monk. My knowledge of scripture had improved since I began my studies, but what worried me about this audience was that they were from India and probably had some knowledge of the *Gita*. I assumed they knew as much if not more than me. Moreover, I had a bit of an inferiority complex because these guys were doing their graduate studies and I hadn't even finished college.

I remember praying really hard beforehand, and being positively surprised that the outcome was much better than I had expected. Riding back on the Greyhound from my second or third trip to Albany, I remember thinking that if lecturing and teaching were this thrilling, I might be able to continue my life as a monk for a long time. It was such a free life. I could study, travel, and lecture while inspiring people in their spiritual lives. What could be better than that? At the same time, I worried that this might just be the initial excitement one experiences in the beginning stages of a new venture. Only time would tell.

Many people join the monastery right after high school or during college. It's easier to take on new challenges in life when you're 19, when life can seem exciting and adventurous. As they approach their mid 20s, they begin to want to experience the world and plan out a career. Hardly a waste of time, they can re-enter society stronger and wiser. Most monks remain in a student/training phase of monastic life, and have the freedom to discontinue their training whenever they like. Some take lifelong vows, but it's recommended to wait until they're in their late 40s or 50s before making such a commitment.

At 27 years of age, I became a monk at a time in my life when settling down had gained its appeal. In those early years, the pressure to figure things out was building—not from my parents or friends, but from within. Could I really live like this? What about getting a job and building a career; and what about saving some money for my old age? Shouldn't I find a life partner and start a family? To add to my dilemma, I had been approached twice early in my monastic life by different women seeking a romantic relationship. Even though I felt uncertain about my commitments, on both occasions I told them that I planned to continue the monastic life, at least for now. One of my teachers told me that every man eventually wants to be a father, and that I could do that by either getting married and having kids or by nurturing others in their spiritual lives. By helping others, I could fulfill my desire to take on the role of a father. These questions continued to haunt me during the first five years. I worried that I might turn 50 and suddenly want a family.

However, I had experienced material life and was pretty convinced that it couldn't bring me the fulfillment that I was looking for. So, even as my mind struggled with these questions, something held me to this lifestyle. I had given up money, relationships, and luxury, but I was happier than ever before. The questions continued to loom in my mind, but with each year it became easier to accept my life path.

I won't pretend that going against the grain of society wasn't difficult. As children in America, our role models are athletes, musicians, and movie stars. Sometimes we pursue a career just to maintain a certain status, whether or not we're happy with that choice. Monkhood is isolated from these choices, as very, very few pursue it in the modern world. There were times when I felt isolated and contrary to society, and had to rely on instinct to keep me going.

I turned 30. I had lived in the monastery for three years, and decided to take two more years to figure out whether I wanted to commit to an extended stay. If I felt uncertain about this lifestyle, I would move out and start a career. Making that resolution and giving myself a timeline was very helpful. A couple of activities sustained me along the way. I started going up to Albany almost every weekend. The student group had grown as they had started inviting their friends. They were coming every single week. They enjoyed learning the *Gita* and I enjoyed exploring their deep questions about the philosophy. I loved having these exchanges. It was nice to surround myself with spiritually inquisitive youth. I once had a lot of the same questions: What is the purpose of life? Who or what is God?

Even they were surprised about the extent of their spiritual pursuits. They would often comment that they never realized that the *Gita* was such a relevant text. These students had not been very religious while they were in India. Being away from their homes and their families sparked a longing to reconnect with their roots. Knowing that I could help them reconnect to their roots and help them answer their spiritual calling provided me with a deep, meaningful, and heart-warming experience.

COLUMBIA UNIVERSITY

My experiences in Albany led me to realize how much I enjoyed interacting with students who exuded such positive energy about life. Even though I was eight to ten years older than most of them, being around them made me feel younger and more positive.

A second opportunity came my way from a friend that I had gotten to know through my spiritual community. His name was Chen and he was an international student from China studying for his PhD in Biology at Columbia University. Having been introduced to the spiritual tradition of India while living in China, he wanted to share it with the Columbia community.

Chen and I arranged to host a discussion program at the university, but after attracting only a small crowd, we decided to organize vegetarian cooking classes. We wanted to introduce people to the concept of vegetarian cooking and how simple, healthy, and tasty it can be. We also wanted to dispel misconceptions that vegetarian foods lack protein or have poor variety. Afterward, everyone would be able to sample the food. I agreed to come to campus every other week to lead the demonstrations. Since I had been on the cooking rotation in the monastery for only a short while, I only knew how to cook a few items. I had to muster up a good amount of courage to lead the first cooking session; what if I burnt something, or didn't spice the food properly?

We conducted the first cooking class in a common kitchen on campus. Five students attended. I engaged the students in cutting up the vegetables, stirring the preparations, and mixing in the spices. We cooked a three-course meal in about 60 minutes: white rice, a spiced vegetable preparation known as sabji, and a popular Indian dessert, made with cream of wheat, called halava. Everything was delicious. There was a small dining table in the kitchen so we all sat together and shared the meal we had just cooked. The students were very grateful for the experience and I was thrilled that I could share the experience with them. The students wanted to continue the program, so we decided to host the cooking classes every other week. At the next session, about 10 students came, and it continued to grow by word of mouth. Everyone was always excited to learn more recipes and to eat more tasty, freshly cooked food.

We caught on quickly that anything food-related is going to be popular with students. At Columbia, some students go to a different event every day of the week for their sustenance. I guess being away from home is more difficult than it seems. I lived at home till I was 27 and then I directly moved into a monastery, so all my food needs had always been taken care of. We realized that this event had tremendous potential because it met so many different needs for the students. It not only provided a freshly cooked meal for them, but it was also giving them tools to cook for themselves. Learning to cook my own food had been such a liberating experience for me, and I also found that cooking could be very therapeutic. Cooking allows one to remove the mind from all the other stresses of life and focus on something more simple and joyful.

The cooking classes also facilitated many students who were experimenting with a vegetarian lifestyle. Vegetarian options can be sparse in the dining hall, and no one can be expected to subsist on salad and pasta for too long. Most of them weren't looking into vegetarianism for spiritual or religious reasons. Rather, many were concerned about the terrible conditions of the slaughterhouses in which meat is produced. They felt reluctant to support an industry in which animals are bred to be killed and treated as nothing more than a product. Many farm cattle live knee-deep in their own fecal matter, a perfect breeding ground for disease. Hens probably get some of the worst treatment. They're packaged together in cages too small for them to spread their wings. Because so many of them are stuffed together within a single cage, they peck away at each other, severely injuring themselves. There's a great quote from Sir Paul McCartney: "If slaughterhouses had glass walls, everyone would become a vegetarian."

British psychologist Richard D. Ryder coined the term Speciesism to describe humans hurting or discriminating against other species. It's not much different than other forms of bigotry, like racism and sexism. Humans have taken the liberty to decide which animals will live privileged lives, and which animals can be legally exploited and abused. According to the Animal Legal and Historical Center, the New York state law against animal cruelty states:

> Animal includes every living creature except a human being. A person who overdrives, overloads, tortures or cruelly beats or unjustifiably injures, maims, mutilates or kills any animal, or deprives any animal of necessary sustenance, food or drink, is guilty of a misdemeanor, punishable by

imprisonment for not more than one year, or by a fine of not more than one thousand dollars, or by both.

All of the above happens in slaughterhouses everyday to millions of animals. However, if one were to mistreat their dog, cat, or any other "pet", they could be fined, imprisoned, or both.

VEGETARIANISM AND THE ENVIRONMENT

Another reason many students have become vegetarian or vegan is because of the environmental impact of the meat industry. When I first became a vegetarian, I had no clue that the meat industry was the number one cause of pollution and ozone depletion. According to a report published by the United Nations Food and Agriculture Organization in 2006, livestock produces 18% of all greenhouse gas emissions. This is more than that produced by the automobile industry. According to the New York Times, livestock in the U.S. produces around 900 million tons of waste each year. All of this waste has a huge impact on the surrounding water, land, and air. Hinduism considers the Earth to be a mother. She gives us everything we need for our nourishment. In return, the very least we can do is to not pollute or exploit her resources.

VEGETARIANISM AND HEALTH

Others are becoming concerned about the health implications of meat consumption. Heart disease, cancer, and stroke—some of the biggest health problems faced by Americans—have all been linked to excessive consumption of animal products. The National Cancer Institute published a report by the Harvard School of Public Health, which states, "Harvard researchers find that red meat consumption is linked to increased risk of total, cardiovascular, and cancer mortality."

It's more than the meat, though; we're also consuming the hormones that have been pumped into the animals. In addition to this, the animal's fecal matter can contaminate the meat during the slaughtering process. The slaughterhouse processes up to a few hundred cattle each hour, so the workers don't always have enough time to prevent fecal matter from getting on the meat. When the contaminated meat is ground up with a bunch of other meat, large quantities can be tainted by the spillage.

THE PROTEIN CONCERN

The biggest concern Americans have about a vegetarian diet is protein. We all know how important protein is for one's overall health. What people are unaware of is that if they eat a variety of fruits, nuts, vegetables, and grains, they will get more than enough protein. All of the amino acids that are needed to create protein are found in the plant kingdom. Vegetarianism has always been a huge part of the Indian/Hindu diet, and no one has ever complained about being protein deficient. My grandfather is in his mid-80s and has never even touched meat, fish, or eggs. He's physically quite fit and has a very sharp memory. The same was true for my great-grandmother, who passed away when she was in her 90s.

Another common misconception arises for those athletically inclined, who feel that they may lose their competitive edge by not taking in meat and the protein that comes with it. Most people aren't aware that there are some very prominent athletes who maintain an animal free diet. Carl Lewis, an Olympic sprinter and long jumper, won 10 Olympic medals of which 9 were gold. He says that his best performances came after he was a vegetarian. David Scott, a triathlete, is the only person to win the triathlon six times. He did this while maintaining a vegetarian/vegan diet. According to New York Times article of January 2012, there is a community of vegan bodybuilders entering the competitive arena. Even some of the top Mixed Martial Artists are turning towards a vegetarian diet. This just goes to show that there is actually nothing deficient about a vegetarian diet. One just has to be thoughtful about it.

BUILDING COMMUNITY
THROUGH COOKING

Bringing like-minded people together was one of the biggest accomplishments of the cooking class. We became a community. In a fast-paced environment like New York City, and in a university as challenging as Columbia, it's not always easy to find a way to meet others who share a common interest. I found it especially satisfying to watch students develop close friendships with each other at our events.

Word about the cooking class spread throughout the campus and the numbers continued to grow. Within four years, we had expanded from 5 to 50 students, and in the next two years, the numbers soared past 100. Many students very honestly admitted that initially they came for the free, tasty meals, but that they kept coming because they appreciated the spiritual atmosphere and the warm community that was developing. On more than one occasion, I overheard students whisper to each other, "I can't believe he does this every week!" On a couple of occasions, students asked me why I do this. In the current present society, no one does anything without getting something in return, but as a monk I saw it as an opportunity to render service and educate people on the values of a proper diet.

I was happy even if students came just for the meal; knowing that I was getting an opportunity to provide much needed nourishment for the body and soul left me quite satisfied. One of the duties of a monk is to live by the principle of selfless and unmotivated service. Of course, it's not easy to always maintain that consciousness. There's always the hope that a lot of people will come and when an event is sparsely attended, it's somewhat natural to feel some disappointment. Over the years I've learned to feel satisfied with however many attend, and I always had to remind myself it's not about the numbers, but the quality of the community.

THE YOGA OF COOKING AND EATING

Students were very fascinated by the idea that cooking with the right consciousness can actually be a type of yoga. I'm not referring to the yoga practice where you try to turn yourself into a pretzel. I am sticking to the original meaning of the term, which arises from the Sanskrit root "yuj," meaning to harness or bind back. Yoga means you are trying to reconnect with the divine. During my vegetarian cooking demonstrations at Columbia University, I explain to students that we should maintain the consciousness that we are cooking for the pleasure of God and that we want to share the food with others.

Knowing that we're cooking for someone else can help remove some of the selfishness we harbor in our hearts. Like yoga, cooking with the right consciousness can purify the heart and mind of negative tendencies. This entails that the cook isn't allowed to taste the food while the cooking is taking place. As soon as students hear this, the immediate response is that of complete surprise. How is it possible to cook without tasting what we are cooking? The truth is that it takes practice. In my tradition, we stick closely to recipes to ensure the quality of food. Since the food is being cooked for the pleasure of God, God should be the first individual to taste it. Perhaps harder than this, the cook isn't supposed to be thinking of eating or enjoying the food while cooking.

As bizarre as all this might sound, this is the method of cooking adopted by those who adhere to the Bhakti or devotional path within Hinduism. One way to express our love for people we care for is to cook for them. So, a similar way to cultivate our love for God is to cook delicious preparations while reflecting on our love and devotion for God. I think most people will agree that a loving mother often prepares the best meals. Every time I visit my folks in Jersey City, my mom cooks for me. Maybe I'm thick headed, but it took me a really long time to figure out why my mom enjoys cooking for me. She gets pleasure from watching me eat what she's cooked. The food she's prepared is imbued with her feelings of motherly love and care. Her consciousness has entered the food and is being transferred to me. That transference of consciousness creates a powerful bond. So, even though she may or may not use the perfect amount of turmeric, hing, or cumin, the most important ingredient is bhakti, or love.

The idea that our consciousness can affect material things may seem a bit farfetched, but we accept this effect taking place with works of art and music. The works are embedded with the consciousness of the particular artists. We can be emotionally impacted by that mood when we experience the art firsthand; whether by viewing it in a gallery or listening to it on our iPod. When we eat, we're not only eating the food and it's ingredients, but we're also eating the consciousness of the cook. Accepting this leads us to ask, "whose consciousness am I eating?"

In the *Bhagavad Gita,* Krishna offers a very salient point: "If one offers Me with love and devotion a leaf, a flower, fruit or water, I will accept it." God isn't looking for elaborate and complicated offerings from the devotees. Instead Krishna is looking for the love and devotion, or the bhakti, behind the offering. Because of this, the offering can't be a product of cruelty, like meat. Such food items are not only unhealthy for our bodies, but also unhealthy for our consciousness.

When food is offered to the Divine or God, it becomes sanctified. In the bhakti tradition, food is offered through devotional mantras that focus our intention. It is understood that God then accepts the offering of food and partakes of it. Because the food comes in contact with the divine, it also adopts divine qualities. In this way, matter is transformed into spirit. When an individual consumes this offered or "karma-free" food, one's mind, senses, and consciousness are purified of such tendencies as greed, anger, envy, and selfishness. One comes simultaneously closer to the divine. Advancing spiritually and elevating one's consciousness can often involve rigorous practices. However, simple endeavors, such as cooking and eating, can also move us closer to that ultimate spiritual goal.

CHAPTER ELEVEN

WHAT GOES AROUND COMES AROUND:

KARMA AND REINCARNATION

Over time, more and more students asked me about my monastic life and about the philosophy that I followed. Not wanting to discuss it during the cooking class, I started a *Bhagavad Gita* discussion group that would allow for a focused discussion of the philosophy and practices expounded in the *Gita*, where the students could feel free to raise concerns, ask questions, and express their opinions about the philosophy.

The teachings most students are fascinated by in the *Gita* are the same teachings that caught my attention when I first started reading the *Bhagavad Gita* in Bulgaria about 20 years ago. Krishna begins by informing Arjuna that he is not the material body, but rather an eternal spirit soul. He goes on to explain that the soul is unaffected by time and that the current life is just one of many.

Not being subjected to birth, old age, disease, and death got my attention. Most people aren't looking forward to these aspects of life. We do our very best to avoid the old age, disease, and death portions of our existence, but to no avail. No one wants to look or get old, so we spend hundreds of billions of dollars on cosmetics and pharmaceuticals to try to preserve our youth and vigor. To keep looking young, we will go to any extreme – stretch, pull, nip, tuck – whatever it takes. Steve Jobs said it so wonderfully, "Even people who want to go to heaven don't want to die to get there."

We experience so much pain in this life when we lose something of value that the pain of death is unimaginable. Losing even little things such as a pair of jeans or a phone can cause pain and disturbance to our lives. A real tragedy, like losing a loved one, can leave us despairing for years. Death rips us away from everything that we hold dear, all at once.

If we consider the process of birth with some thoughtfulness, I'm pretty sure we'd want to avoid that too. Getting your whole body and head squeezed out over hours and hours seems like nothing less than torture. It's no wonder that we come out of the womb and into the world screaming at the top of our lungs. Chapter two of the *Bhagavad Gita* explains:

> *The soul exists forever in the present, having no birth or death. The soul is the oldest, without beginning or end, and is not killed when the body is killed...As a person exchanges old clothes for new, so the soul abandons old bodies to enter new ones.*

Krishna dedicates the entire first section of chapter two to explaining this concept to Arjuna and to all the readers. The basic point that Krishna wants to drive home is that we have been identifying ourselves with something we're not; we think of our lives as temporary and material, when in fact we are spiritual and eternal. It's a very difficult paradigm to digest, even if you were raised with a belief in the soul. Basically, it's telling us that when we're looking into a mirror, we're not seeing the actual person. The real person is sitting within the body. The body is often described as a vehicle with the soul as the driver. A vehicle can't function without the driver. The soul is seated in a vehicle made not of metal, but of flesh and bones. The eyes are like the headlights and the arms and legs like the wheels, which allow for motion.

It's explained within the *Upanishads* (Hindu scriptures) that the soul is one ten-thousandth the size of a tip of hair. The *Bhagavad Gita* describes the soul as "invisible and inconceivable…unbreakable, insoluble, and can be neither burned nor dried." The Upanishads also explain that the soul resides in the region of the heart. On more than one occasion, I have been asked, "If someone gets a heart transplant, are they also getting a new soul?" The answer is no. The soul is in the region of the heart but doesn't move if the heart is removed. The soul is the spiritual spark that creates consciousness. It can also be said that it is consciousness itself. Without the soul, the body is just a lifeless lump of matter that starts decaying and loses all attractiveness.

However, recognition of our spiritual identity doesn't translate into indifference towards our own or others' bodies. The body is very important and can't be neglected. It takes the soul to its next destination. That destination can either be another material body or liberation from the karmic cycle of birth and death.

Of course, liberating the soul from being entangled in the body is no easy task. It takes a regulated and committed spiritual endeavor involving meditation, yoga and the overall elevation of one's consciousness towards others and the environment around us. Those who have realized that the material body isn't permanent will commit to transcending this cycle of birth and death. When I had this realization, I started taking small steps towards reuniting the soul with God. I knew that I had a long way to go, perhaps even several lifetimes, but felt it was a worthwhile endeavor. Our deep rooted connection to the material world, desire for fame, prestige, and wealth keep us bound to the world of matter and force us to take birth again and again to fulfill these aspirations.

Many teachers believe that we've existed in the material universe for millions of births. Each birth is determined by our karma. The word karma literally means "activity." It can be understood through the old adage, "what goes around comes around," or the biblical equivalent, "as you sow, so shall you reap."

Karma can be divided into a few simple categories – good, bad, individual, and collective. Depending on one's actions, one will reap the fruits of those actions. The fruits may be sweet or sour, depending on the nature of the actions performed. Fruits can also be reaped in a collective manner if a group of people together performs a certain activity or activities. Everything we say and do determines what's going to happen to us in the future. Whether we act honestly, dishonestly, help others or hurt others, all of it is recorded and manifests as a karmic reaction either in this life or a future life. All karmic records are carried with the soul into the next life and body. There is no exact formula that is provided for how and when karmic reactions will appear in our lives. One might be able to avoid paying their taxes or getting away with a crime they have committed for the time being, but according to karma, no one gets away with anything.

A karmic reaction, good or bad, may or may not manifest in the same life. It may manifest in a future life. It's also possible to get hit with a few reactions— positive or negative—at the same time. The simplest analogy I can think of for how karma works is that of a credit card purchase. You make the purchase now, but don't get the bill for thirty days. If you made several purchases during one billing cycle, then you will receive one big bill.

Often, when something goes wrong in our lives, it can feel senseless. We can just be left bewildered without any answers. When my family lost its business and all its possessions and had relocated to Bulgaria, I asked myself why this was happening. I came up with three possible answers:

1. God is cruel for letting things happen the way they are.
2. Things are happening completely by random chance.
3. In some way, I had a hand in my own suffering, even if I wasn't able to recall what I had done.

I didn't like option two because I just couldn't accept that things were moving about randomly. I always felt there had to be some kind of order to the universe. Since I grew up believing in God, I was ready to wholeheartedly accept option one because this option allowed me to point a finger and express my anger and frustration at someone who I had worshiped all my life. Hindu sages and scriptures pointed towards the third option, but that was even more difficult to accept than the others because it meant I couldn't really point a finger at anyone other than myself. It was a little frustrating. I was being encouraged to take responsibility for my own actions and not to place blame on others. It explained that each of my previous lives had impacted my subsequent lives and is probably affecting my current life.

The natural question that arises is "Why am I getting punished for something from a previous live if I can't even remember it?" Of course, we don't ask ourselves why good things happen to us. We simply accept the good thinking we deserve it or that we've earned it. The most important lesson to learn is that we can become more mindful of our present actions to prepare our families and ourselves for a more prosperous future, both materially and spiritually.

Karma doesn't mean we should feel indifference towards the suffering of others. Our attitude should never be "too bad, it's their karma." Rather, we should always strive to feel sympathy and compassion for others.

The Hindu tradition deals with life in a cyclical manner and not a linear one. Just as we go through the yearly cycle of four seasons and the daily cycle of day and night, so birth, death, and rebirth is the cycle of life for all species. One life isn't enough to break through the cycle of birth and death. We need multiple lives to learn all the lessons life has to offer and correct the mistakes we've made. Students appreciated the idea that ones entire fate, for eternity, isn't judged by an individual's actions from just one lifetime.

When some of us learn about reincarnation, we become curious about our past lives. I am sometimes asked whether it is ever possible to remember these experiences. I encourage my students to first consider whether they really want to remember their past lives. The pain of dealing with the hardships of our current life is difficult enough. We can only imagine how long we would actually survive if the weight of our previous lives' pain and suffering were compounded onto our psyche. For the most part, it's probably a good thing that most people don't remember what happened in previous lives, so that we can move forward in our present life. However, recollections are possible, and some individuals have benefitted from a past-life regression session, which helped them to understand how a pain in the current life was connected to an incident in a previous one.

REINCARNATION RESEARCH

Increasing evidence is becoming available about the same people being reborn. Dr. Ian Stevenson, former head of the Division of Perceptual Studies at the University of Virginia School of Medicine, explored the paranormal in his research. His team conducts studies in which very young children, usually between the ages of two and seven, remember very specific details from their previous lives. Many of the prominent case studies on reincarnation are from Asian countries where the philosophy is widely accepted, but they discovered many American cases. Some details these children were able to recall from a previous life were: their legal name, occupation, names of family members, details of their houses, and the manner in which they died. Dr. Stevenson and his team collected as much detail as possible by interviewing the children and the family members about previous lives recollections and then attempted to verify these details. In addition to using memories from previous lives, some children were born with birth defects that were hypothesized to be connected to some violent episode leading to their demise in a previous life. The birth defects and their connection to the previous life could be verified through medical and postmortem records.

In 2005, there was an American case in which a boy began to have violent nightmares at around two years old. In the dreams, he recalled dying as a fighter pilot in a plane crash during World War II. He was able to remember his name, the aircraft carrier on which he was stationed, and the location in which the airplane was shot down. His family was even able to get in touch with the sister of the pilot, who was still alive at the time, and a co-pilot. The parents of this child didn't initially believe in reincarnation, but were forced to consider that their son had lived a previous life as a World War II fighter pilot.

Over the last eight years that I've been conducting the Gita discussions at Columbia University, most of the participants are of a non-Indian, non-Hindu background. In 2002, I became the Hindu Religious Life Advisor (chaplain) at Columbia. It turns out that Columbia, like other universities, has never had a Hindu representative, and so I was the first. A few years later, Hindu students from New York University also invited me to lecture and requested for me to become their chaplain as well. As the years progressed, I found myself going to campus almost five days a week to assist with events or to meet with students about their personal or spiritual life.

CHAPTER TWELVE

TRANSCENDING THE
QUARTER-LIFE CRISIS

In my fifth year as Columbia's Hindu chaplain, I came across the term "quarter-life crises." During a conversation over lunch, a student told me about it, and then towards the end of the school year another student gave me a book called, *Quarter Life Crisis: The Unique Challenges of Life in Your Twenties* by Alexandra Robbins and Abby Wilner. Similar to a mid-life crisis, it refers to the plight of students in school or just out of college trying to figure out what they want to do with the rest of their lives. When I ask college seniors if they know about their plans after they graduate, they give me a consistently similar response: "I have no idea."

The uncertainty and panic of a quarter-life crisis can be caused by a combination of factors. All of the facilities and conveniences a college campus provides will no longer be available: on-campus residential housing, eating facilities, medical and counseling facilities, security, and clubs and organizations where students can meet other students. It can be even more intense if you can't find a job after graduating, or if you find something in your field and realize that you don't want to do this for the rest of your life, leaving you to regret all of the time and money spent on something you no longer want to pursue. Moving back home with your parents isn't the most attractive option, as it can feel a bit restrictive, and it can make graduates feel like they're regressing. Not everyone is affected by these concerns, but even one or two of them can push students to act in extreme ways to resolve their situation. The Huffington Post published an article about college women engaging in sexual acts with wealthy older men in exchange for money to pay off their student loans.

I believe the root of the quarter-life crisis is that right from our childhood we've been driven and pushed to achieve material success and social status. The equation we've been memorizing all our life is that material possessions, position, and success equals happiness, yet there are so many people who get all of this and still feel empty inside. We've almost completely ignored our spiritual needs. We've run full speed ahead, pedal to the medal, and we never stop to consider what's really going to make us happy. Material things can only give us so much. They can only provide temporary satisfaction for the senses, for the physical body and mind, but they do little for the heart and soul.

It's quite amazing that we've hardly ever been seriously encouraged to pursue the needs of the soul, and we may even have been discouraged to do so. It's no wonder that so many people hit a brick wall.

The fifth chapter of the *Bhagavad Gita* explains:

> *One whose happiness is within, who is active and rejoices within, and whose aim is inward*

is actually the perfect mystic. He is liberated in the Supreme, and ultimately he attains the Supreme.

Taking care of the needs of the body and ignoring the needs of the soul is like watering the leaves, fruits, and flowers of the tree, but forgetting to water the actual root.

It's only a matter of time before we come face to face with a quarter or mid-life crisis. The crisis happens because we lose sight of who we really are, and we can't figure out what we're supposed to do. The sooner in life we're able to implement into our lives spiritual practices of meditation and yoga with the intention of understanding the true nature and needs of our soul, the better chance we have of preventing such a crisis from hitting us in the face.

The wisdom of the *Gita* encouraged me to focus on the more permanent things in life, such as understanding the eternal nature of the soul, and how the purpose of life is to re-establish my lost relationship with God. Once we're en-route to re-establishing that relationship, many other aspects of our life become clearer. The problem is that we get so caught up with all of our material affairs that we wait for something to go wrong before we take action. The recommendation of the *Gita* is to make sure each day we incorporate some meditation and reflection into our lives. It could prevent a "quarter-life" crisis from happening, and if it doesn't, these practices can provide us with the coping mechanisms we will need to get through it.

Soon after becoming the Hindu Religious Life Advisor, I started coming to the campus five days a week to teach vegetarian cooking classes, lead multiple discussion groups and lead meditation sessions. Students started to approach me to discuss their personal lives. The most common topic of discussion was relationships, usually ones that were broken or over. Already under the high-pressure demands of studying at an Ivy League school and juggling their extracurricular activities, breaking up with a loved one would knock the wind out of them.

The most intense situations came up when students had discovered their partner was cheating on them. When someone first came to me about this, I was shocked and didn't really know how to respond. They looked completely shattered and their feelings of betrayal and devastation reminded me of someone experiencing a death in the family. It left me speechless for a while.

One student walked in on her boyfriend with another girl at a party. She said that she was so shaken up and disturbed that she's glad she was able to make it back to her dorm. She had to take the subway home at 4:30 in the morning. It took her months to get over it. I knew I just had to hear her out completely and try my best to empathize with her situation, which of course, wasn't easy. There is no fixed way to respond to these cases because each person and situation is unique. In a three-semester stretch, three students approached me about the exact same thing, and I came to realize that cheating must be a common phenomena. It left me wondering how many more must be going through the same situation and if they had someone to confide in.

Many international students have to adjust to the challenge of being not only away from their home, family and culture, but also their country. It gets harder and harder, especially if they don't have any relatives in the United States. Hindu students coming from India sometimes made their way into our vegetarian cooking classes or *Bhagavad Gita* discussions. They were so relieved to be able to eat a traditional Indian meal, especially if they were vegetarian. There aren't many satisfying vegetarian options for people who have been raised with an Indian palate, and these students usually can't afford to eat out because they're living on loans. Most of them never studied the *Bhagavad Gita* while in India, but being so far from home and feeling homesick drives them to explore the very culture they left far behind. There is an interesting dynamic between the Hindu students that come from India and ones that grow up here. They might look alike, but are culturally very different and usually not very compatible with each other. International students usually stick together because they share common struggles and can talk about how good life was back in India, how they miss their families, and how different American culture is from their own.

People have asked me how am I contributing to society as a monk. I tell them that I'm trying to bring spirituality into people's lives and that I do my best to be available to people if they need to talk about personal or spiritual issues. Whether I'm on campus talking to a student, or at a local coffee shop talking to a working professional, I see that basically everyone is struggling with similar issues. Most people want to talk to me about their purpose in life or the difficulties they're experiencing in personal relationships. Many individuals I talk to are looking to figure out which direction in life they should pursue professionally. For a student, it's trying to decide between majors or where they should live. For a working professional, it's trying to understand which direction to go in after investing five, ten, fifteen years or more into a specific field of work.

I've also noticed that people are never struggling with just one thing. They come to me with one problem, but after a couple of talks all kinds of other things begin to surface. One woman came up to me after one of my talks in a yoga studio and said she wanted to tell me about a spiritual experience she'd had. I gave her my card and a few days later she called me. After sharing with me her experience, I found out that she was suffering financially because her husband stopped paying alimony and that she was incredibly stressed out.

After another lecture at a yoga studio, a man said that he would like to speak with me because he was really confused about life and didn't know what to believe. We decided to meet at a local vegetarian restaurant. I thought we would talk about his spiritual beliefs and practices. He began instead by telling me about a stressful business venture and that they had not been able to break even after almost a year. He didn't know what the future held for his business and wasn't sure how the rent was going to get paid. Then he told me that he had been in a relationship for many years that just didn't seem to be working out, compounding the other stresses he was dealing with on a daily basis.

Sometimes, people don't hesitate to get right into their problems. It used to surprise me because, for the most part, these are people I barely know. Other times, people won't bring out their real issues until they have reached a certain comfort level with me. They want to know that I'm listening and that I can understand what they're going through before they go deeper and open up. After hearing them out and asking questions to further understand the situation, I usually recommend what helped me during the different obstacles I faced in life: spiritual teachings and practices that I used to strengthen my spiritual foundation. Too often, we think that by acquiring money, friends, and influence, we can build a secure future, and to some degree this is true. However, the problem is that all of these things can go as easily as they come. Watering the leaves, fruits, and flowers can make them look clean and shiny, but is doesn't truly nourish them from the inside.

We live in such a fast paced environment that people hardly have time for each other. One student told me that she hadn't seen her best friend for four months even though they both attended Columbia. Even at the monastery, the monks are sometimes so busy that we have to schedule appointments with each other, often a week in advance, just to be able to sit down and talk. I therefore encourage individuals to create time in their busy lives to water their souls with spiritual practices. If the root of our spiritual lives is strong, then we will be able to withstand even the most turbulent storms that life has planned for us. Too often, we start the watering when the storm has already arrived. Better late than never. However, if we can start the watering process as soon as possible and start strengthening the root when things are still smooth, we can be prepared for the turbulence.

I also help people understand that oftentimes, the mind has a tendency to magnify the problem and make it seem more severe than it actually is. I can offer this advice because I've seen my own mind do this on many occasions and have given the same advice to myself. Many times, just by discussing the situation or challenge, people are able to gain a more balanced perspective on the situation. I recommend people to turn to the *Gita* and mantra meditation to see if it helps pacify the mind. For some, the effects have been amazing. One person was so excited to share with me that chanting the mantra was helping her get rid of not only her insomnia, but also her cigarette patch. This was the first time someone had come to me with such radical results. Others told me that it has helped them calm down, relax, and get a better idea of how their mind works and why it panics when it doesn't really need to.

Once while flying back to New York from Los Angeles, I went to the back of the plane to ask one of the attendants for a glass of water. As I turned to walk back to my seat, I noticed that one of the attendants had a curious smile on her face and had indicated that she wanted to talk to me. Given that I was wearing orange robes, I knew she probably wanted to know a little about my life.

Very politely she said, "I don't mean to offend, but I was wondering if you're a monk."

I said, "Yes, I'm a Hindu monk."

"Is that part of Buddhism?" she asked.

"No, it's different from Buddhism…I'm a Hare Krishna monk," I responded.

She said, "I thought the Hare Krishna was Buddhism."

She then turned towards her colleague and asked if she knew that Hare Krishna was Hinduism. Her colleague acknowledged that she also didn't know the connection. She then pointed a finger toward her own forehead to ask me to explain the markings on mine. I explained that they represent the footprint of God and that it symbolizes our humility before God by keeping his feet on our head. "I think I would rather be on God's back" she commented.

Another of her colleagues then approached from the front of the plane to ask me to explain the markings. I asked the first attendant if she would like to explain which she promptly did. She said she was very happy that she had learned something new. After that, I returned to my seat.

These are very common questions that I get asked in public places. I would always prefer that people approach me and ask about my attire and tradition than just form an opinion, which may not be supported by fact. Sometimes, the questioner is polite, other times challenging. It's just part of the package that comes with being a monk in the city.

When I first moved into the monastery, I never imagined that I would become so involved with the people of the world. However, my kind of involvement was very different from when I had a day job. First of all, I wasn't looking to make money from my endeavors. It is very fulfilling because I know I am helping people. In order to make myself accessible to people, I found myself using all the technology I had thought I was leaving behind. A few students had suggested that since I'm in touch with so many college students, I should get a Facebook account. This was back in 2006. I had thought it was some kind of dating site, so I was reluctant to sign up. Eventually, I had a friend open an account for me, but afterward I felt a bit self-conscious telling people I had an account. Every time I told students to find me on Facebook, they would smile with a wondrous look. I knew they were thinking, "What's a monk doing with a Facebook account?" The smiles continue to this day, but at the end of the day it has helped me to stay in touch with students who have graduated over 10 years ago and who are in all different parts of the world.

CHAPTER THIRTEEN
MORTALITY AND TRANSCENDENCE

There is a funeral home across the street from our monastery next to the drag queen bar. I see a hearse pull up in front of the home a few times a week. The driver opens the back door, pulls out a coffin, and rolls it in. I've seen restaurants, delis, and shops come and go on my New York block, but the one establishment that remains unaffected by the economy is the funeral home. When I see the coffins, I can't help but remember that the person in that casket was a living, breathing individual with family and friends. What must it be like for those left behind? What was their experience in the moments before their departure?

We have a subconscious tendency to deny our mortality. Even though death is happening all around us, we never think that we will be affected by it. Driving by a cemetery might make us a little reflective, but somehow we're not able to connect that to our own life. It's like the elephant in the room. However, it's natural for us to be fearful of our own mortality. It reminds me of a conversation that takes place in the famous Hindu epic *Mahabharata* between a wise king and a realized sage. The sage asks the king, "What's the most amazing thing you've seen in life?" The king replies, "The most amazing thing I've seen is that death is taking place everywhere, but no one ever thinks it's going to happen to them."

Death is a terrifying experience. The entire body and all of its functions come to a halt. Everything we hold dear is on the verge of being stripped away from us. We are so devastated when we lose something as trivial as a cell phone or a wallet, so how can we possibly imagine losing everything, all at once! Death can show up at the door without giving any kind of advance notice. So is there anything we can do to prepare for that final moment of our lives, or will we be helpless victims?

One of my teachers says, "Life is the preparation and death is the final examination." We can't ward off death. The death rate is and always will be 100%, but the more we prepare, the better equipped we will be in dealing with the inescapable truth of the situation. Death is not a test we can cram for the night before.

The Hindu scriptures explain that we come into this world with a certain number of breaths and the countdown begins the moment we exit the womb. Since we don't really know when it's going to happen, every moment should be lived preparing our consciousness for the final moment. This doesn't mean that we're constantly wandering around depressed thinking of our demise. It means living life such that we're constantly endeavoring to create a balance between our material and spiritual lives. The wisdom found within the Hindu tradition of India can provide us with a less fearful, brighter outlook on our own mortality, while teaching us to prepare for our final moments. These teachings can also help us better deal with the loss of a loved one.

Chapter Two of the *Bhagavad Gita* enlightens us with a few passages that provide us with a beautiful and broad perspective on life, death, and our ultimate existence:

> *As a person exchanges old clothes for new, so the soul abandons old bodies to enter new ones.*

> *The soul cannot be cut by weapons, burned by fire, drenched by water or withered by wind.*

These verses alleviate our most fundamental concern, the fear of ceasing to exist. The *Gita* explains that the only thing about us that deteriorates and dies is the body. The real person is the soul, which continues to live on without being affected by any of the elements of this world, including time, which is ultimately responsible for diminishing the life of all matter. Time, however, has no effect on the spiritual self or soul. This is not our first life and it will not be our last. The soul is eternal and it will continue to exist even after the demise of this body. Knowing this can provide some solace about our own existence and the existence of those we care for. It also teaches us that in order to properly prepare for that final exam, we need to engage in spiritual acts, which will help us to realize the nature and reality of our soul, and simultaneously help distance us from the bodily concept of life.

REMEMBERING THE DEPARTED

A Columbia University alum who had been regularly attending my *Gita* discussions, introduced me to one of her friends while visiting my temple. She mentioned that her friend is going through a lot and that it would be nice if I could speak with her. I shook hands with her friend, gave her my email address, and told her to reach out to me. Sure enough, a few days later she emailed me requesting to meet. It was during the winter months and conditions were blizzard-like with heavy snowfall. Nevertheless, she came to the temple to talk. I could tell by the look on her face that she had been going through a difficult time.

She told me that she had recently lost her grandfather and was devastated by the loss. It was especially difficult for her because her grandfather was in a different country, so she was not able to be with him during his last moments. She was as close, if not even closer to him than her parents and he had loved and cared for her dearly. In her words, "I was his little princess." I had never witnessed anyone mourn so intensely over the loss of a grandparent. While talking about him, she would get teary-eyed and needed to take breaks so she could regain her composure. All she could talk about was how much he cared for her and for everyone in their family, even if the family members didn't reciprocate his affection or were hurtful towards him. He was selfless. Not only that, he was incredibly spiritual.

Her grandfather was born in India but had migrated to New Zealand in his youth. He developed a very successful business there and had become a prominent member of the community known for his generosity. Before his death, he went to India and organized an eye surgery camp in the Gujarat region, where over 1,000 poor people had the opportunity to repair their eyesight. Afterward he told his nephew, "My soul can now rest in peace." Around 5:00 a.m., a week after the camp was over, his wife saw him sitting on the living room sofa on her way out for a walk. He was wearing a new set of clothes and had the *Bhagavad Gita* in his lap, his head hanging down. He never put on fresh clothes that early in the morning. Somehow, he knew this would be his last night. The *Gita* explains, "Whatever one thinks of at the time of death, that state one will attain." Even though he had achieved tremendous material success and prestige in his lifetime, he had made sure that he not only knew how to live in this world, but also how to leave it.

Initially, we met a few times a month, but over time our conversations slowed to once a month and gradually, months would go by before we would talk. Yet even after an entire year, her grandfather was always our main topic of discussion. She carried a picture of him on her phone, in a locket, and in a ring. I told her she was incredibly fortunate to have had someone like him in her life. Many people don't get a chance to experience that kind of love.

Hearing her speak about him would make me reminisce about my own grandmother back when we were still living in Kanpur, India and how much she loved and cared for me. She would do anything for me and I preferred being with her over my own parents. I was very close to my grandmother as a small child, but when she passed away from the world I had already been in the United States for over 12 years. Though my attachment had diminished over time, my dad cried like I had never seen him cry before. His father had passed away when he was only seven years old, so he was quite close to his mother. He regretted that he couldn't be with her when she passed away.

Death is a very difficult topic to deal with. We want to know that our loved ones are in a good place. There was little doubt in my mind that my friend's grandfather had reached a wonderful destination. His death had driven her to seek shelter in the Gita and in spirituality, neither of which had held any interest before. Even when her grandfather had tried to talk to her about the *Gita* when she was little, she only expressed disinterest and boredom. He never pushed, but instead told her, "One day, I hope that you pick up the *Gita* and you come to understand." Since his death and our conversations, the *Gita* has become a crucial component of her everyday life and it has helped her move forward. She now understands the positive impact the *Gita* had on her grandfather's life. It not only taught him how to live in the world, but also how to leave it.

CHAPTER FOURTEEN

CELIBACY AND THE CITY

Most people I encounter are quite fascinated by the idea of monks living in Manhattan. Most monks live away from a busy city in a place that allows for focused meditation and reflection on spiritual life. Wouldn't a city like New York, a place seen by many as the height of materialism, seem quite counterintuitive to a monk's lifestyle?

It all depends on the monk's purpose. If they are aspiring to focus only on their own meditation and spiritual practice, then a busy city environment can definitely be counterproductive. However, if they choose to reside in a city so they can help people, then there's no better place. Within the Bhakti tradition of Hinduism, it is recommended that monks who can live in the city spend some time there. The city is where people are most stressed and need the most spiritual guidance. It's a very intense place where everyone is constantly scrambling from one activity to another, keeping themselves busy, and often times leaving their spiritual pursuits by the wayside. The Bhakti tradition teaches that making oneself available to assist others develops one's own compassion, which is a very important tenet of Hinduism.

The city can actually push one to greater levels of focus in one's meditation practice. There are so many distractions everywhere, and to prevent oneself from getting sucked into ubiquitous materialism, one really needs to take greater shelter of one's meditation and other spiritual practices. For example, when one is driving at high speeds, one needs to be more attentive, otherwise the chances of an accident are much greater.

I'm more comfortable in a city environment than some of our monks. After all, I was born in Kanpur, which is an extremely busy and industrial city, and then lived in New Delhi and Los Angeles. When I first moved to New York, I actually found it to be an exciting place. I like busy places. People, cars, trucks, and other city noises don't really bother me.

In 2003, our monastery moved to Third Street in what's known as Alphabet city, an area within the Lower East Side. It is referred to as Alphabet City because the Avenues are named for letters of the alphabet, going from Avenue "A" to "D". In the not too far past, Alphabet City was known for illegal drug activity and violent crimes. One person I talked to said that "A" stood for "alright," "B" for "bad," "C" for "crazy," and "D" for "dead." Since we were between "C" and "D," we were somewhere between crazy and dead.

The area has been gentrified in the last 15 years and is quite safe. We lived in this apartment for two years and had no problems whatsoever. The rare thing about this apartment was that we had a backyard, which is unheard of for Manhattan housing. It even had a tree! I spent an entire summer sitting under that tree reading the "Mahabharata," one of two major epics of India.

In 2005, we moved to our current location on First Avenue near Houston. It was by far the busiest location. From the outside, the building looks like just another New York brownstone—you could honestly walk right past it and not notice anything special.

The natural question arises, what in the world are monks doing in a place like this? At the time, there were about 15 of us and we all woke up between 4:00 and 4:30 a.m. Our morning meditation started at 5:00 a.m. To refresh ourselves from the night's sleep, everyone is required to shower, put on a clean set of robes, and then enter the temple room for the meditation and worship. According to the teachings in Hinduism, the mind has the easiest time focusing during the early morning hours. The mind responds to all the stimuli around us, including people, traffic, noises, and activity in general, but there's not a whole lot of this activity going on at 4:30 a.m.

For many novice monks, the biggest challenge usually is getting up at 4:00 a.m. everyday. The only time you get to sleep in is if you're sick, if you just couldn't fall asleep the night before, or if you had a program that went late into the night. When the alarm goes off that early in the morning, the first thing your mind experiences is disbelief. The spontaneous reaction is to hit the snooze button, but you know you can't hit that button too often because it never feels good to show up late. In the Mumbai temple, where I first explored monastic life, the latecomers are required to write the Hare Krishna mantra 108 times. That takes up almost an hour. Moreover, everyone sees you sitting there during meditation writing it out. That system works pretty well out there. We thought about implementing it here, but decided against it because we felt it would be too strict a rule for the Western culture.

In any case, someone's going to flip the light switch and for most of the monks it's pretty much impossible to continue sleeping when that happens. Next, there's a mad rush to the bathrooms. You're only allowed to lock the door of the bathroom if you're sitting on the toilet. While brushing your teeth and showering, the door is supposed to stay unlocked so others can use the bathroom to brush their teeth or use the toilet. This "not locking the toilet door" is specific to our monastery because we have limited bathroom facilities. Even if you're on the toilet, it's hard to be peaceful knowing that there's a couple of guys waiting outside the door. The rule of the morning shower is that it has to be quick. Longer showers can be taken during the day. I guess to some, it can feel like something between camp and boot camp.

The morning service is very similar to what I experienced in the Mumbai and Vrindavana temples. The only difference was the number of people that attended in India was between 50 to 100 compared to 5 in New York. It's an incredibly powerful, devotional, and spiritual way to start the morning. It's more energizing than a double espresso, and the experience stays with you the entire day.

Since we live in a community, everyone learns how to do pretty much everything. All novice monks learn how to cook, clean, assist with altar service, play the different instruments, sing, and lecture. This enables one to get absorbed in the culture and provides steady engagement for the mind and intelligence. In the first couple years, the monks learn the different activities and gradually, according to their propensities, they will increase their engagement with one or more specific services.

The next big challenge for most of us is living so close to one another. Most of us have shared a room with a sibling, but now you're sharing a space with grown men. We have a couple of large open spaces and a couple of small rooms where we live. Those spaces function as our bedrooms, study rooms, and dining rooms. We have a couple of futon beds and a couple of small desks. Everyone uses thin, foldable, air-filled sleeping mats and a sleeping bag, all of which can be put away in the morning, leaving the area nice and spacious.

The sleeping part gets interesting, especially when people have different sleeping habits and patterns. Some might have a tendency to snore, while others like to get up even before 4:00 a.m., which means their alarm clocks will wake the others up. I like to use a fan, but others don't. Some can sleep through a train wreck, but others of us are extremely sensitive to noise and light.

We don't have a perfect system, but things have worked out somehow. It's not that we always get along and everything is fine and dandy. We get to know each other really well. We all know each others' habits, likes, dislikes, and idiosyncrasies. Everyone knows what will make the other person happy and what will push their buttons. This is where we learn to not only tolerate each other but to try to appreciate and heighten our sensitivity to each others' needs and concerns. We all come from very different cultures, ethnic and religious backgrounds, so building and maintaining relationships requires a lot of work. It's understood that not everyone will get along perfectly with everyone else, but most do have decent friendship with one or two others in the monastery. We start the day off together at 4:00 a.m. and are together till lunch at 2:00 p.m., so we end up spending more time together than most families or couples.

It provides us with a wonderful opportunity to assist each other in advancing spiritually. We also understand from our previous teachers that by cooperating and developing friendships with each other, we can overcome our tendency to judge others. It becomes especially helpful for when we engage with people who live outside our monastery, whose lives are very different from ours.

The close proximity of our co-existence also provides us ample opportunity to practice the wonderful and much needed art of forgiveness. Since we live so close together, rubs will naturally take place. Our scriptures teach us that we can't grow spiritually unless we tolerate and forgive. If a disagreement takes place between two monks, the culture of the monastery recommends they ask forgiveness from each other and try to see their own faults in the situation. If it's still not working out, a third, more senior monk, will mediate between the two. The world and all the people in it are going to throw so many situations at us that if we don't learn to forgive and let go, we'll get crushed by the burden of all the hard feelings we're harboring in our hearts. It's a constant reminder that all relationships are a work in progress.

In order for someone to even move into the monastery, they need to have been practicing our rules for about a year. Otherwise, the transition would be way too difficult. Even young men who spend a few nights a month in the monastery before they move in can still find life in the temple to be a culture shock. All of a sudden, the freedom to do what you want when you want to is no longer there. Like a boarding school, the monastery has a strict schedule for its residents. There's no television. We don't go to the movies. Most of the food we eat is cooked in the monastery and all of us practice celibacy. In addition to this, all monks are required to abstain from all alcoholic beverages, caffeinated products, meat including fish and eggs, and gambling. Those who consider moving in are totally aware of the rules and regulations, and are eager and enthusiastic to experience the monastic way of life. It's hard to say how long that enthusiasm will last. I've seen some people last just a few days, while there are some who have been joyfully at it for over 40 years.

CELIBACY

Celibacy is the rule that presents the biggest challenge for monks at any monastery. Most of us are in our early to mid 20s, 30s, and 40s and have had at least one, if not multiple, relationships before moving into the monastery.

One of our resident monks was in a very serious relationship with someone for a few years. Their families had gotten to know one another and they had discussed engagement and marriage. It was his most serious relationship, but his spiritual calling became so intense that he left his partner and moved into the monastery. He said it was very tough for him to break it off, but he couldn't neglect the calling to find God. He has lived in the monastery for around nine years.

Another one of our monks, stayed with us for about a year before returning to Texas to reconnect with his former girlfriend. I myself had been involved with someone six months before going to the monastery in Mumbai.

When we move into the monastery, we are told to see all women as our "mothers." This is suggested to help us maintain a proper and respectful attitude towards the opposite sex. When I first heard this, I thought it was a brilliant way to maintain the right consciousness when interacting with women. It doesn't always work, though—the mind very quickly lets you know "this is not your mother."

Hindu monks aren't supposed to have any contact with women to prevent temptations rising from within their own hearts, not because women are seen in a negative manner. Monks in India have little or no contact with women, and will even avoid shaking their hands. Within the culture of India, women usually won't approach or have detailed interaction with those in the renounced order of life. To keep things simple, many monks in India live in areas where they can avoid the general public. It would be practically impossible to practice monastic life in America the way it is done in India.

However, I choose to live and practice monastic life in the West, and more specifically in the Lower East Side of New York. The city does everything but support a celibate lifestyle. Here, if I didn't shake a woman's hands, she might be offended or think that I'm living in the Stone Age. Most of my lecturing engagements are at a university, yoga studio, high school, or someone's home, so the audience typically includes men and women. Often times, I'm approached by attractive women seeking advice and spiritual guidance and I have to remind myself to be very cautious. I have known and have heard of monks, not only from my tradition, but also from other strands of Hinduism and Buddhism, who become attracted to and couple with someone they were guiding. The regular interaction leads many of the monks to decide to get married.

Then there's the issue of hugging. In the West, hugging is part of the cultural norm, and is seen as a friendly gesture of affection. We grow up hugging our friends, guys and girls. I often develop friendships with the people I'm lecturing to or guiding, so it's just a matter of time before a woman will want to give a friendly embrace. If I see it coming ahead of time, I'll quickly stick my hand out for a handshake, but often times it happens so fast that I can't do anything about it.

Once, after lecturing at a yoga studio, a lady gave me a hug and then smilingly said, "I'm not sure if I'm supposed to hug you."

I replied, "I don't hug women, but can shake hands."

"Why?" she asked. I could tell she was a bit offended. For the next 20 minutes I tried to explain to the best of my ability why monks don't hug women. Eventually she accepted it, but something told me she wasn't totally satisfied.

Once while walking around the campus of Union Theological Seminary with some friends from the student body and faculty, I saw my friend Denise, a woman who had gotten to know me through lectures and even hosted me for her Thanksgiving dinner with her family.

When I realized it was her, I called out, "Hey Denise!" She turned around with a big smile on her face, gave me a huge hug, and planted a kiss on my cheek. It was the first time anyone had kissed me in my 13 years as a monk.

"I don't know, is it okay to hug a monk?" she asked, looking a little perplexed.

Smiling, I nonchalantly replied "no," and everyone except her burst out laughing. I think she was a bit embarrassed, but no one took it that seriously. A couple of times, older ladies that I have become close friends with have told me "I know I'm not supposed to hug you, but I'm going to do it anyways." It didn't bother me because I felt they were treating me like their son. Having to constantly explain why I don't hug women gets a little tedious. I try to avoid it as much as possible and many women do pick up on it.

I was surprised to learn that the Jewish and Islamic cultures have similar practices when dealing with the opposite sex. Once after an interfaith event, I went around the room shaking hands with all the faith leaders. When I went to shake the hand of the Orthodox Rabbi's wife, she promptly informed me, "I don't touch other men." It was an awkward and uncomfortable moment. I felt stupid for not knowing. However, I was relieved to learn that other traditions also follow a similar belief. I suppose there has to be some level of awkwardness and discomfort when two very different cultures collide, but hopefully the collision doesn't cause too much damage.

There's absolutely nothing wrong with two people who care for each other to show affection for one another. Krishna explains that sex life is not contrary to sacred principles. However, some individuals, like myself, make a voluntary decision to abstain from such relationships in order to dedicate all of their time and attention to going deeper into their spiritual life and helping others do the same.

Nearly all resident monks will eventually choose to get married and re-enter the working world within a few years. One of our aspirations is to learn about the urges and tendencies that control our minds and lives and the only way to really do this is to distance the self from them. Learning to leave them aside for a period of time provides us with a glimpse of freedom that can be quite liberating. Those who feel they can't continue the lifestyle because of celibacy or because they want to pursue a career are encouraged to move forward. The years they spent in the monastery help to create a strong spiritual foundation, which will stay with them as they engage with the world.

WHEN A MONK LEAVES THE MONASTERY

The monks in our monastery don either white robes or saffron (orange) colored robes. Since the color saffron represents stronger commitment to the monastic life, novice monks are requested to put on white robes for a few years until they feel settled and able to maintain the lifestyle for some years to come. In India, saffron is traditionally seen as a life long commitment, but here in the West, where the culture doesn't support the lifestyle, saffron is given to the more committed with the understanding that the individual still has the flexibility to leave the monastery if he so chooses.

Most of the time, it's not easy for a monk to transition back into the outside world. Often times they feel embarrassed that they couldn't make it. Some novice monks usually enter the monastery with the romantic idea of being a lifelong monk. People moving in with this conception sometimes acts immaturely and feel themselves to be more advanced than they actually are. So, when they have to move out, they feel as if they have failed.

Newer monks and even veteran monks are often affected when someone leaves the monastery. It makes them question whether or not they can continue. If they were friends with the individual that left, they might experience some loneliness and loss of company when their friend leaves. The biggest shakeups happen when a more senior monk, who has been around for 5, 10, 15 or more years, decides to leave. That really makes everyone question their own capacity to sustain in this environment. There can be a feeling of panic, especially if they expected this individual to remain in the order till death.

Back in December 2011, the senior-most monk from our monastery decided to leave. It deeply affected the entire community, both monks and householders. He had lived as a monk for almost 25 years and was 52 years old. He was the one who gave me and many others tremendous guidance when I first started visiting the New York temple and he was even the one who suggested that I visit India to go deeper into my spiritual life. He started the monastery in Manhattan that I moved into after my six months in India, and we lived in the monastery together for about 12 years before he decided to go in a different direction. During his travels, he had met someone and wanted to pursue the relationship. We had believed that he was fully satisfied within the monastic order. Later, after he had transitioned out, he admitted that these feelings had been there for quite some years. It became difficult for him to say anything because of the enormous pressure that was placed on him due to his seniority and position in the community.

Many monks that don the saffron cloth feel this pressure. Even if they haven't taken a formal lifelong vow of renunciation, people start to treat them as though they have. After a while, you start feeling you have committed to a lifetime even if you know that it might not be a permanent thing. I don't know about monks in other traditions, but 99 percent of all those who enter the monastic order in the Western countries will eventually get married. Still, senior monks are treated as though they will continue for the rest of their lives in the monastic order. The community can feel let down when a monk decides to transition out. Feelings of shame and embarrassment sometimes cause the monk to delay their move, increasing the stress and pressure he may be feeling.

His transitioning out shocked me in a way I wasn't expecting. I would regularly get news of monks in monasteries in other parts of America and India who after spending 10, 20, or 30 plus years in the monastic order, were making the shift, but that never deterred me in my determination. I had no deep emotional connection with any of them and so it didn't affect me.

This, however, was very close to home. It was the first time I realized that human emotions are quite unpredictable and that there's no such thing as overcoming our feelings. At any time, the desire to have intimate companionship could arise within the heart and one would have to confront it. Even though the idea was always mildly in the back of my mind, I had become so busy teaching, lecturing, counseling, and traveling that I never seriously considered it. However, this made me rethink my options in a way I never had before. Is it possible these feelings could surface in my heart some years down the line? I wasn't getting any younger. Would it be better to transition out now and figure things out before I got much older? I told my parents and many of the community members that although I wasn't going to rush into anything, I had become open to the possibility of making a transition. My parents, being the good, caring, and enthusiastic Indian parents that they are, immediately offered to help me find someone. I told them I would let them know when I became sure of it myself.

It was a difficult time, but I now had the opportunity to take inventory and get in touch with my emotions. I'd kind of just accepted that I would live like this for the rest of my life. Starting your material life again in your mid-30s, 40s, or even 50s isn't ever easy, especially if you want to have kids and build a career. Many monks have found it hard reintegrating into the social culture of society, especially after having spent a long number of years in the monastery. The first year outside is usually difficult, but they always settle in and figure things out within a year or two. Many of the monks that have passed through our particular monastery have gone on to finish college, become school teachers, yoga instructors, lawyers, and businessmen. According to the original Vedic tradition of India, the initial stages of monastic life are meant to be a training ground. It has always been understood that only a few would be able to carry on till the end of their lives.

Monks were traditionally not allowed to mix with their families. Rather, they would leave their town or village and wander through the forests and jungles from town to town and never return. It was quite a dangerous lifestyle. The point was to develop complete dependence on the shelter of God. You took nothing with you except the clothes on your back and a begging pot. Afterward, the monk would travel alone village-to-village, passing through dangerous forests and jungles. It was not recommended for women, but there were always female monks who broke these restrictions. My grandmother left home and five young kids behind to live in a monastery for a period of time. She was in her mid-30s and was a very devoted and spiritual lady. My grandfather went to bring her back. My mom tells me that the night before she passed away, she got up at night and went back to the monastery where her guru, who was also a lady, resided, and she passed away from the world at around 4:00 a.m., the most auspicious time of the day according to Hinduism.

I have tried off and on to maintain some contact with our monk alumni, but it's difficult because most of them move out of New York City. They're looking for a fresh start, and a new surrounding provides an opportunity to figure things out. Some monks end up spending time with their families as they try to get clarity on the next stage of their lives.

Like most spiritual and religious organizations, the members of our spiritual community maintain our monastery and temple. The Vedic system proposes a system of spiritual care wherein the working members of the community provide financial assistance and the volunteering of their time and skills to help maintain the temple. In return, the monks and priests are supposed to physically maintain the temple and provide spiritual teachings and support along with spiritual counseling as and when required. This system of reciprocal service between the monks and householders is the system under which our temple and monastery function.

Most people in the world see monks as lifelong celibates who have given up all connection to family, worldly enjoyment, material desires, and aspirations. This, however, is not the case. Material desires and ambition don't vanish because one has shaved one's head and put on robes. That can only happen after many lives of disciplined spiritual practice. Leaving everything behind is a very powerful experience, even if it's only for a few months or a few years. Most who have gone through the experience will usually say it was one of the best times of their life.

CHAPTER FIFTEEN

GOING BACK TO CALI

When I left for Bulgaria, I didn't bother to stay in touch with anyone except for one high school friend. We usually caught up once a year by phone. However, I had asked him to keep my exact situation from the rest of our friends, and he honored my request. It was too complicated to explain. No one just randomly moves to a foreign country. But my dad made a sudden decision, and I followed him. He urged me to stay in school, but I told him I had made up my mind to come and work with him.

Moving to Bulgaria seemed easier than dealing with all the things that were falling apart. In Los Angeles, I didn't have money to go out with my friends anymore. I couldn't ignore them, and I didn't want to tell them that we were about to lose everything. Even when we moved back to the U.S., I didn't want to reach out to them. I thought about them from time to time, but my life was still unstable and I didn't want to reestablish the connection. Then four years after living in New Jersey, I entered the monastic order. There was no way I was ready to explain this!

It wasn't until around October of 2009 that my friend told me over the phone that our high school friends were still asking about me and wondering where I was. They heard rumors that I went to

Europe, but that was all. He told me about recent Facebook comments where they were trying to figure out where I was. He reminded me that our 20th high school reunion was coming up. But I knew there was no way I would go to that. Having a shaved head and wearing orange robes, I would stick out like a sore thumb. I would have to explain the last 20 years of my life to everyone. However, I told him to go ahead and give out my contact information and Facebook page so they could be eased into understanding my life.

The very next day, the phone rang while I was at a meeting in my office. I picked up to hear a voice yelling out my name and saying, "It's Carl; do you remember me?" I was shocked—Carl was one of my closest friends from high school. He said he had searched extensively on the internet to locate me, but couldn't find me because I'd taken on a new spiritual name. We only spoke briefly because I was in the middle of a meeting. But by the end of the conversation, I felt a bit emotional.

The next day I got a friend request on Facebook along with a contact number from another friend named Joseph. As soon as I called and introduced myself, he just started laughing and then I started laughing. For the next minute, we just laughed. I know this sounds kind of crazy, but it was the kind of laugh that says, "I can't believe we're talking after all this time." We must have talked for the next hour and a half just catching up about our lives.

During the week, I got bombarded with friend requests on Facebook from all of my high school friends. Everyone's profile picture included a picture of his or her spouse and kids. They started uploading pictures from our high school years. It was such a strange experience to be reconnecting with people I was once so close to. The last 18 years had been like a roller-coaster ride. Looking at those pictures made me wonder if the past had really happened. It brought back throngs of memories.

The following week, I got in touch with a few more friends. They insisted that I come for the reunion. I considered it, but still had reservations. I told them I would look at my schedule and get back to them. Deep inside, I knew I had to go. It wasn't by chance that I was reconnecting with them just six months before our 20th reunion. I knew it was a rare opportunity for me to build a bridge between the first part of my life and my current one. I could re-establish relationships that were important to me. I could share my experiences and hear about their own journeys through life. I knew that emotionally this would be a very healing experience, and it would give me that much needed chance to process a lot of what had happened.

After I told them I was coming, they went out of their way to make me feel welcome and accommodate the different needs and standards of my monastic life. Carl insisted that I stay with him. Another friend named Victoria, who's always good at getting people together, arranged for me to have vegetarian food for my entire visit.

In May 2010, I found myself on my way to Los Angeles. Initially, I stayed with my aunt, but a day later my friend Carl came to pick me up. He took me on a short tour of Glendale and even took me up to my old house. Nostalgia was kicking in. I had been back to LA to visit some relatives, but this trip was different. Some friends had arranged for me to deliver a lecture about my philosophy and practice at their church on Friday evening. It was during my lecture, as I was standing behind the podium, that I began to notice several of my old high school friends sitting in the audience. I had to focus hard, because every time I recognized someone in the audience, I would recall the various exchanges I had had with them while in school. Talking to them after the event felt surreal.

I met more of my friends and some of my teachers at the reunion that Saturday. I spent the entire evening telling my story over and over again. I was moved when some of my friends told me that the main reason they had attended the reunion was because they heard that I was going to be there. I was surprised that I connected so well with some classmates that I never really knew, and so weakly with some people I was once close to. Life had taken everyone on a unique journey.

The reunion was a weekend long event, and Sunday's portion was going to take place on campus. I was quite excited to visit the campus after so long, where I had so many great memories with my friends. We had even spent weekends there, playing in the gym or just hanging out. We would meet up at the cul-de-sac by campus on Saturday evenings and figure out where to go from there.

One of my friends invited me to a basketball game the guys from our class put together. I hadn't played in such a long time and was pretty out of shape. I went to the gym, but I had my robes on. At first, I just watched everyone warm up and shoot hoops. I decided to start shooting around, and then one of my friends said he had an extra pair of sneakers he could lend me. Another friend, who had become the high school gym teacher, told me he could give me a jersey. I put on the jersey and sneakers and was ready to play basketball.

I hadn't been to a gym for almost 17 years, so I felt out of place. We played for about an hour. Most of us were really out of shape, huffing and puffing as we ran up and down the court. We constantly had to sub for one another. During the game, the ball slipped from my hands when I tried to pass it down the court and went into the basket. One of my friends yelled, "That's swami power!" He was suggesting that my meditation practice had something to do with the ball accidentally going into the basket.

After the game, I walked around the high school campus for a while meeting old friends and getting introduced to their spouses and kids. I remembered my first day at the school in 1986. It sure didn't feel like two decades had gone by, and I definitely didn't feel like I was almost 40 years old.

After the reunion ended, I had another few days left in Los Angeles. I met more old friends during that time. There were people who were close friends of our family that we had cut ourselves off from. I decided that I would meet as many of them as I could.

"Reunion" became the theme of the whole trip. It was so much better than I could have imagined, and since then I have continued to stay in touch with quite a few of my friends. I even went back to LA the next summer to see them again. I enjoy living in New York—it's where I found my spirituality and where I became established as a monk—but, like most people, there is a special place in my heart for my hometown and the dear friends I have there still.

EPILOGUE

O King, as small particles of sand sometimes come together and are sometimes separated due to the force of the waves, the living entities who have accepted material bodies sometimes come together and are sometimes separated by the force of time.
(Srimad Bhagavatam 6.15.3)

This passage speaks to my life journey. I could have never imagined that by the time I was 21, I would have lived in three different countries—India, the United States, and Bulgaria—and have had three very different sets of life experiences. Coming back to the United States after Bulgaria was a new beginning. Little did I expect life to thrust me to live in a monastery and then back to New York where I would dedicate the next 13 years to serving people as a spiritual guide, chaplain, and counselor.

If I step back to reflect on how many people have come and gone in my life, it's easy to feel like a grain of sand with no control of my surroundings. It's unsettling to imagine how many more times in my life I will be carried away from the people closest to me, like the sticks and planks in a river. Even after so many separations—from cousins, aunts, uncles, and grandparents in India, to my friends in Los Angeles—it's never ever an easy experience.

The amazing thing about this constant change is that it has happened for hundreds, thousands, perhaps even millions of lifetimes. How many families have we had, and how many more will there be? How many more do we want to have and lose? The *Gita* and other Hindu texts have forced me to wrestle with these questions. The texts can sometimes seem as if they are suggesting a certain level of indifference towards family and friends, but they never encourage irresponsibility towards those who have helped and cared for us. In our current lifetime, it's so important to value the relationships we have been given because each is helping us grow, even if it's difficult.

As each day passes, I find myself becoming closer and closer to my parents. More and more, I feel as though I am developing a friendship with them. We're a three-person unit, and together we've gone through so much gain, loss, happiness, and distress. My gratitude and appreciation for all they've gone through and the tremendous sacrifices they have made for each other and me increases each day. They have supported me in all facets of my life and continue to do so in my monastic practice. My hope is that I will be able to repay a little of what they've done. I know I can never match their dedication and commitment, but I can try my best to support them.

We try to avoid thinking about being separated from a loved one, but deep down most of us worry about losing people we care for. While that will happen, we can find solace in understanding that everyone has an eternal existence. Beyond the endless cycle of life and death, the one relationship that has always been with us and will never leave us is the relationship we have with God. It is my aspiration, and I hope it will become the aspiration of many, that as we move through life's turbulent waves and get tossed around, we will endeavor every day to become more resolute in our determination to move closer in our relationship with the eternal divine, who I call Krishna.

ACKNOWLEDGEMENTS

Without the blessings and inspiration from many of my teachers, I wouldn't be where I am today and this endeavor would not be possible. This book would still be on my hard drive without the tireless and dedicated efforts of Chelsea Pula who edited and brought structure to the book. I would like to express my deepest gratitude to Christopher Fici who encouraged and nudged me to keep writing and who was my sounding board throughout the entire process. My heartfelt gratitude to Olia Saunders for designing the book cover. I would also like to thank Liz Gallagher for planting the seed of publishing into my head, which is now beginning to bear fruit.

A special thanks to many of my friends who provided valuable feedback and support on multiple levels: Ashish Shah, Simon Christopher Timm, Hilary Hanson, Silvana Saieh, Ghanasyam Das, Sarah Sherman, Varun Soni, Sree Sreenivasan, Roopa Unikrishnan, Deena Guzder, Rowen Barber, Pragnesh Surti, Hannah Perls, Phil Goldberg, Ajay Shrivastav, Contessa Gayles, Damodar Mahajan, Jahnabi Barooah, Deepal Bhula, Genevieve Price, Shashi Raina, Tina Ling, Joni Yung, Bisakha Ray, Jake Siemaszko, Murli Gopal Das, and Gaur Kumar Das.

REFERENCES

1. *Bhagavad Gita As It Is,* Text courtesy of The Bhaktivedanta Book Trust International, Inc.www.krishna.com. Used with permission.

2. *Srimad Bhagavatam,* Text courtesy of The Bhaktivedanta Book Trust International, Inc.www.krishna.com. Used with permission.

3. *Caitanya Caritamrta,* Text courtesy of The Bhaktivedanta Book Trust International, Inc.www.krishna.com. Used with permission.

4. Prime, Ranchor. *Bhagavad Gita: Talks between the Soul and God.* London: Fitzrovia, 2010. Print.

5. Dasa, Gadadhara Pandit. "Why Suffering and Spirituality Go Hand-in-Hand." *The Huffington Post.* TheHuffingtonPost.com, 05 Dec. 2011. Web. 01 July 2013.

6. Barker, Kenneth L., and Donald W. Burdick. "Luke 23:34." *The NIV Study Bible.* Grand Rapids, MI: Zondervan Pub. House, 1995. 1584. Print.

7. Barker, Kenneth L., and Donald W. Burdick. "Matthew 18:22." *The NIV Study Bible.* Grand Rapids, MI: Zondervan Pub. House, 1995. 1466. Print.

8. Dasa, Gadadhara Pandit. "The *Bhagavad Gita*: You Are Not Your Mind." *The Huffington Post.* TheHuffingtonPost.com, 19 June 2011. Web. 01 July 2013.

9. Dasa, Gadadhara Pandit. "The Birth of Krishna: When God Came To Earth." *The*

Huffington Post. TheHuffingtonPost.com, 22 Aug. 2011. Web. 01 July 2013.

10. Dasa, Gadadhara Pandit. "Radha: The Feminine Nature of God." *The Huffington Post.* TheHuffingtonPost.com, 04 Sept. 2011. Web. 01 July 2013.

11. Barker, Kenneth L., and Donald W. Burdick. "Matthew 5:43 - 5:45." *The NIV Study Bible.* Grand Rapids, MI: Zondervan Pub. House, 1995. 1446-447. Print.

12. Web blog comment. *Goodreads.* N.p., n.d. Web. 1 July 2013. <http://www.goodreads.com/quotes/search?q=Dalai+Lama+compassion>.

13. Dasa, Gadadhara Pandit. "A Splinter in the Mind: The Matrix Through Hinduism." *The Huffington Post.* TheHuffingtonPost.com, 03 Oct. 2012. Web. 01 July 2013.

14. Dasa, Gadadhara Pandit. "The 33 Million Gods of Hinduism." *The Huffington Post.* TheHuffingtonPost.com, 06 Aug. 2012. Web. 01 July 2013.

15. Bittman, Mark. "Rethinking the Meat-Guzzler." *The New York Times.* N.p., 27 Jan. 2008. Web. 1 July 2013.

16. Pan, An, Qi Sun, Adam M. Bernstein, Matthias B. Schulze, JoAnn E. Manson, Meir J. Stampfer, Walter C. Willet, and Frank B. Hu. "Red Meat Consumption and Mortality." *Harvard School of Public Health News.* N.p., 12 Mar. 2012. Web. 01 July 2013.

17. Pilon, Mary. "Vegans Muscle Their Way Into Body Building." *The New York Times*. N.p., 4 Jan. 2012. Web. 1 July 2013.

18. Dasa, Gadadhara Pandit. "A Hindu's Call To Vegetarianism." *The Huffington Post*. TheHuffingtonPost.com, 09 Oct. 2011. Web. 01 July 2013.

19. Dasa, Gadadhara Pandit. "The Yoga of Cooking and Eating." *The Huffington Post*. TheHuffingtonPost.com, 03 June 2011. Web. 01 July 2013.

20. Stevenson, Ian. *Twenty Cases Suggestive of Reincarnation*. Charlottesville: University of Virginia, 1974. Print.

21. Stevenson, Ian. *Where Reincarnation and Biology Intersect*. Westport, CT: Praeger, 1997. Print.

22. *Reincarnation - Airplane Boy (abc Primetime)*. 2011. YouTube. *YouTube*. YouTube, 10 July 2011. Web. 01 July 2013. <http://www.youtube.com/watch?v=Uk7biSO zr1k>.

23. Dasa, Gadadhara Pandit. "*Bhagavad Gita*: You Are Not The Body." *The Huffington Post*. TheHuffingtonPost.com, 20 Mar. 2012. Web. 01 July 2013.

24. Dasa, Gadadhara Pandit. "Karma: What Goes Around Comes Around." *The Huffington Post*. TheHuffingtonPost.com, 11 Nov. 2011. Web. 01 July 2013.

25. Dasa, Gadadhara Pandit. "Transcending the Quarter-life Crises." *The Huffington Post.* TheHuffingtonPost.com, 10 Aug. 2011. Web. 01 July 2013.

26. Fairbanks, Amanda M. "Seeking Arrangement: College Students Using 'Sugar Daddies' To Pay Off Loan Debt." *The Huffington Post.* TheHuffingtonPost.com, 29 July 2011. Web. 01 July 2013.

27. Dasa, Gadadhara Pandit. "Death: The Elephant in the Room." The Huffington Post. TheHuffingtonPost.com, 06 July 2011. Web. 01 July 2013.

ABOUT THE AUTHOR

Gadadhara Pandit Dasa (also known as Pandit) is a monk, lecturer and the first-ever Hindu chaplain for Columbia University, New York University, and Union Theological Seminary. He speaks at the nation's leading universities, yoga studios, and retreat centers, inspiring audiences with India's spiritual wisdom. His unique approach combines teachings of the ancient classic, *Bhagavad Gita*, with popular Hollywood movies.

Pandit spoke at a recent TEDx conference at Columbia University and was featured in the NPR piece "Long Days and Short Nights of a Hindu Monk." He appeared in the PBS Documentary on the *Bhagavad Gita*, as well as The New York Times. He is also a regular contributor for the Huffington Post.

Find Pandit online:

Email: contact@urbanmonkbook.com
Website: urbanmonkbook.com
Facebook: www.facebook.com/panditg
Twitter: twitter.com/nycpandit

Made in the USA
Lexington, KY
28 July 2013